Spirituality and Morality

INTEGRATING PRAYER AND ACTION

Edited by
Dennis J. Billy, C.SS.R.
Donna L. Orsuto

PAULIST PRESS
New York/Mahwah, N.J.

Cover design by James F. Brisson.

Cover photo courtesy of Scala/Art Resource, NY. Andrei Rublev's "Trinity of Uglic," Rublev Museum, Moscow, Russia.

Library of Congress Cataloging-in-Publication Data

Spirituality and morality : integrating prayer and action / edited by Dennis J. Billy, Donna L. Orsuto.
    p. cm.
    Includes bibliographical references and index.
    ISBN 0-8091-3611-2 (alk. paper)
    1. Spirituality—Catholic Church.   2. Christian ethics—Catholic authors. 3. Christian life—Catholic authors. I. Billy, Dennis Joseph, 1953. II. Orsuto, Donna L., 1956- .
  BX2350.2.S628   1995   95-37835
  240—dc20   CIP

Published by Paulist Press
997 Macarthur Boulevard
Mahwah, NJ 07430

Printed and bound in the
United States of America

Contents

*To our students
at
The Vincent Pallotti Institute
of the Laity*

Batter my heart, three-personed God; for You
As yet but knock, breathe, shine,
and seek to mend.

John Donne

Editors' Preface

As Catholic theologians both of us have experienced first-hand the difficulty of integrating the material we teach with the lives we live. Rather than giving in to discouragement, or losing hope or, worse yet, encouraging the same in others (especially in our students), we decided to take pen in hand, articulate our concerns, rally our colleagues behind us, and do something about it. This book is the result of our concerted efforts, however meager, to address some of the issues that emerge at the interface of theology and lived Christian experience.

Our purpose here is to examine how the theological disciplines of spirituality and moral theology interact and influence each other along a variety of intellectual and popular fronts. To accomplish this task, we asked a select group of Catholic scholars, many of whom also happened to be our friends, to address different aspects of a relationship which has admittedly become as wide and as varied as theological reflection itself. Like us, each of these scholars has grappled in his or her own life with the tensions involving the spiritual and moral dimensions of Christian existence. These tensions, which, for the most part, have established the contours of the relationship between spirituality and moral theology, are studied in their historical, theological, vocational, social, personal, and liturgical contexts. In one way or another, each of these dimensions has felt the repercussions of what has been termed "the marriage, divorce, and remarriage" of the Western Christian spiritual-moral tradition.

In varying degrees and with subtle shades of emphasis, the eight chapters of this book stress the importance of integrating theology as an academic discipline (in this case, moral theology) with life in the Spirit. As their content and approach indicate, maintaining a vital and healthy rapport between the fields themselves and the theologian's relationship to them is indispensable for the sound development of the Catholic theological tradition. Although the chapters represent original pieces of research in their own right and may be treated as such, the sequence in which they appear reflects our firm belief that personal integration in these areas flows first and foremost from a sound experience of the Church's theological tradition. As the following summary demonstrates, the earlier chapters focus more heavily on the historical and theological foundations that provide the condition for the possibility of reintegrating spirituality and morality, prayer and action, in our lived experience of the faith, while the later ones presuppose these insights and focus more readily on more practical and personal concerns.

In chapter one, for example, Dennis J. Billy, C.SS.R. uses Dostoyevsky's *The Brothers Karamazov* (1880) as a point of departure for the various historical factors that must be taken into account when discussing the rocky and, at times, volatile relationship in Western Christianity between spirituality and moral theology. Aptly entitled "The Unfolding of a Tradition," this chapter provides a brief historical sketch of the tensions encountered in the Church's theological tradition and is followed by a helpful "counter-discourse" that outlines in ten theses the directions future discussions on their relationship should take.

In chapter two, "The Dynamics of Conversion," Brian V. Johnstone, C.SS.R. asserts that all of theology must be understood as a reflection on conversion. By examining the conversion narratives of two very different and, one might go so far as to say, "unorthodox" Catholic "saints"—i.e., Edith Stein (1891–1942) and Bartolomé de Las Casas (1474–1566)—he highlights the importance of authentic *metanoia* for the life of the Church and its ongoing theological tradition. This enables him to outline the different, albeit related, tasks assumed by spirituality and moral theology in maintaining and developing the health of that tradition.

Lynda Robitaille claims in chapter three, "A Sense of Vocation," that teachers of spirituality and moral theology must be motivated by a profound sense of call. She begins by arguing that an intellectual mastery of the discipline, important as it is for good teaching, does not itself guarantee an effective implementation of the goals of theological education. She further asserts that the person who teaches in either or both of these disciplines must seek to communicate the tradition in the context of his or her personal relationship with God. Only by maintaining this delicate balance between academic excellence and the convictions of a living faith will teachers make a difference in the lives of their students.

In chapter four, "Listening to God Within," Christopher O'Donnell, O. Carm. discusses the many challenges facing the Church in today's post-Christian society. As a way of responding to the world's current crisis of religious experience, he explores the richness of the Christian spiritual tradition and shows how the Christian at prayer has the unique opportunity of sharing in the intimate life of the Trinity. Referring to pertinent texts from Eastern Christianity and the Carmelite tradition within Western spirituality (especially Teresa of Avila and John of the Cross), he shows how authentic prayer embraces every aspect of human existence and seeks, at one and the same time, both to listen to God's call and to respond to the profound moral implications that flow from it.

In "The Church at Prayer," Jan Michael Joncas claims that liturgy fosters the spiritual life of the believer and provides the entire Church community with significant moral insights for the good of all humanity. Basing himself on a wide array of magisterial teachings and liturgical texts, he shows how authentic ecclesial prayer cannot be divorced from its moral dimensions. In his opinion, the liturgy provides a concrete medium through which a person can encounter the transcendent, experience solidarity with humanity, and foster his or her continued growth in the Spirit. It also promotes a common foundational vision for ethical behavior, critiques the destructive elements of the surrounding culture, and celebrates prominent instances of social transformation.

In the sixth chapter, "Forming Right Relationships," Kevin J. O'Neil, C.SS.R. focuses on the close link between love of God, love of neighbor, and love of self. Basing himself on contemporary psychological theories of human and moral development, he underscores the social dimensions of human existence and demonstrates how an authentic love of others is actually a manifestation of an authentic love of self. Using a series of helpful biblical, philosophical, and theological texts, he goes on to show how human friendship points to the intense yearning each of us has for an intimate friendship with God. In his view, Christian morality becomes enfleshed when a well-balanced spirituality nourishes all the relational aspects of human existence and keeps them fundamentally intact.

In chapter seven, Herbert Alphonso, S.J. spells out "Docility to the Spirit" in terms of discerning the extraordinary in the ordinary. Starting from the contemporary thirst for integrated living, he shows how the apostolic ideal of "finding God in all things" can only be realized through a personal experiential process of growing inner freedom, which is at the core of authentic docility to the Spirit. In this context he highlights the contemporary relevance of the pedagogy of the Ignatian Spiritual Exercises which are geared precisely to this goal. Applying this pedagogy, then, to the crying need for discernment in today's Church and world, he offers the practice of the daily "consciousness examen" as the concrete means of living that docility to the Spirit which discerns the extraordinary presence of God in the ordinary of daily life experience.

Finally, in chapter eight, "The Saint as Moral Paradigm," Donna L. Orsuto examines the challenges posed by postmodern society to authentic Christian discipleship. Using the metaphor of a rationally-controlled world gone awry, the likes of which has been enshrined for generations to come in the science fiction thriller "Jurassic Park," she highlights the need for Christian witnesses whose very lives firmly embody and communicate on a pre-theoretical level the truth of the Gospel. She looks to those who have been particularly attuned to the presence of God in their lives to provide us with a paradigm for moral living that will inspire us to deepen our love of God and neighbor.

Taken together, these chapters address the relationship between spirituality and moral theology from a number of important vantage points: history, conversion, vocation, personal prayer, liturgy, right relations, docility to the Spirit, and disciple-ship. While they in no way exhaust the possible list of topics that would be relevant to the discussion of the relationship between spirituality and moral theology, they make substantial headway into what, by most counts, remain largely unchartered waters. Certain that others will one day venture well beyond the limits of our present horizons, we make this modest contribution in the hope that it will in some way help our readers to orient themselves aright and steer a steady and stable course through the uncertain currents and hidden ambiguities that lurk beneath the surface of all theological knowledge.

Last but not least, we would like to take this opportunity to thank in a formal way all who have worked with us on this project and who have helped us to bring it to completion. Conceived as it was from our own experience of and frustration with the many tensions in which spirituality and moral theology are presently conceived and taught, this project would never have gotten off the ground without the interest, support, and commitment of those who responded to our initial query, and whose hard work and prayerful insights have given sound, professional substance to this book. Their contributions have not only reaffirmed our own commitment to further collaborate efforts in the area of spirituality and morality, but also given us a deeper understanding of the specific role that Catholic theologians are to play in the Church's ongoing understanding of its rich spiritual theological tradition. To all of them, to our communities at Sant' Alfonso and The Lay Centre at Foyer Unitas in Rome, and to all of our students, past and present, at The Vincent Pallotti Institute of the Laity, we wish to extend our sincere and heartfelt thanks.

Dennis J. Billy, C.SS.R.
Donna L. Orsuto

Contributors

Herbert Alphonso, S.J., a Jesuit priest from India, holds an S.T.D. from the Gregorian University in Rome. He is Dean and Professor of Spiritual Theology and Ignatian Spirituality at the Institute of Spirituality, Gregorian University.

Dennis J. Billy, C.SS.R., a Redemptorist priest from the United States, holds a Th.D. from Harvard University Divinity School and an S.T.D. from The Pontifical University of St. Thomas. He is an associate professor of the history of moral theology and Christian spirituality at the Alphonsian Academy in Rome.

Brian V. Johnstone, C.SS.R., a Redemptorist priest from Australia, has an S.T.D. from The Catholic University of Louvain, Belgium and holds a chair of special moral theology at the Alphonsian Academy in Rome.

Jan Michael Joncas, a priest of the Archdiocese of St. Paul and Minneapolis, holds an S.L.D. from The Pontifical Liturgical Institute of St Anselm in Rome. He is an assistant professor of theology at the University of St. Thomas in St. Paul, Minnesota.

Christopher O'Donnell, O.Carm., a Carmelite priest from Ireland, holds an S.T.D. from the Gregorian University in Rome. He teaches at the Pontifical Milltown Institute in Dublin, specializing in ecclesiology, mariology, and spirituality.

Kevin J. O'Neil, C.SS.R., a Redemptorist priest from the United States, holds an S.T.D. from the Alphonsian Academy in Rome. He is an assistant professor of moral theology at Washington Theological Union in Washington, D.C.

Donna L. Orsuto, a Catholic laywoman from the United States, holds an S.T.D. from the Gregorian University and teaches at that university's Institute of Spirituality. In Rome, she is also the director of The Lay Centre at Foyer Unitas, an international center for laity who are studying at the ecclesiastical universities and research institutes in Rome, and The Vincent Pallotti Institute of the Laity, a European branch of Education for Parish Service.

Lynda Robitaille, a Canadian Catholic laywoman from Vancouver, British Columbia, holds a J.C.D. from the Gregorian University in Rome. She is a lecturer in canon law at St. Paul University in Ottawa, Canada.

Editors' Notes

Unless otherwise stated, all English quotations of Scripture come from *The New American Bible*, 1st ed. (Cleveland/New York: The Catholic Press, 1970).

Unless otherwise stated, all English translations of Aquinas' *Summa* come from Thomas Aquinas, *Summa theologiae*, with Latin text and English translation, Introductions, Notes, Appendices and Glossaries, 61 vols. (London/New York: Blackfriars/ Eyre & Spottiswoode/ McGraw-Hill, 1964–81).

Unless otherwise stated, all English translations of Vatican II documents come from Austin Flannery, ed., *Vatican II: The Conciliar and Post Conciliar Documents*, revised ed. (Boston: St. Paul Editions, 1988) [hereafter referred to as Flannery, ed., *Vatican Council II*].

Chapter One

The Unfolding of a Tradition

DENNIS J. BILLY, C.SS.R.

The complex historical questions surrounding the ongoing relationship between Christian spirituality and morality cannot be resolved in a short, introductory essay of this kind. Rather than even attempting to do so, it makes much more sense to limit the chapter's scope at the very outset and to try to identify those specific concerns that still need further study and clarification. To accomplish this task, I will use a well-known literary classic to point out the general importance of studying the relationship between spirituality and morality. This fictional point of departure will lead us into a discussion of the meaning of the terms "spirituality" and "moral theology" themselves which, in turn, will set the stage for some necessary historiographical considerations and a brief historical overview of their interaction over time. A series of "theses" or "hypotheses" will follow, the intention of which will be to delineate as far as possible the course further discussions on the topic should take. Through these and other means, I hope to examine the ongoing relationship between Christian spirituality and morality in an adequate historical context and with appropriate room for contemporary applications.

The Morality of Immortality

The opinions of Ivan Karamazov, one of the central characters of Fyodor Dostoyevsky's great Russian novel, *The Brothers*

Karamazov (1880), provide a helpful way of introducing a "field-encompassing" study of this kind.[1] The second son of a petty and morally depraved nineteenth-century Russian landowner, Ivan gains a reputation for himself while attending the university "by selling short 'stories' of street incidents to different newspapers under the signature of 'Eyewitness.' "[2] A withdrawn and sullen young man, he becomes an avowed skeptic at an early age and feels no qualms whatsoever about writing and publishing pieces about events which never happened or on serious subjects, the precise conclusions of which he has absolutely no faith in whatsoever. A reliable observer relates how, on one occasion, Ivan lets down his guard and reveals his true colors:

> "He [Ivan] added…that if you were to destroy the belief in immortality in mankind, not only love but every living force in which the continuation of all life in the world depended, would dry up at once. Moreover, there would be nothing immoral then, everything would be permitted, even cannibalism. But that is not all: he wound up with the assertion that for every individual…who does not believe in God or in his own immortality, the moral laws of nature must at once be changed into the exact opposite of the former religious laws, and that self-interest, even if it were to lead to crime, must not only be permitted but even recognized as the necessary, the most rational, and practically the most honorable motive for a man in his position."[3]

Ivan's thesis is quite simple: take God and immortality out of the picture and the entire moral edifice collapses. Once this happens, a person must be content with whatever shelter he or she can find amidst the ruins left behind. As Ivan's own life attests, such a course of action can be personally disastrous. His rationality of self-interest creates a deep chasm between his publicly stated positions and his own private sentiments. Having lost his faith in God and his own immortality, he sees no reason why he should be bound by anything other than that which suits him. He alone stands at the center of his moral universe and sees no one but himself in the movement of the stars above.

Even though Karamazov overstates his case, only half believes it himself, and carries his conclusions to outrageous extremes, he puts his finger on an important (and often overlooked) link that exists between Christian spirituality and Christian moral behavior. A relationship between reason and grace, between ethics and belief, between the law of nature and the law of the Spirit, *does* exist and should not be taken lightly. With the proper qualifications, his otherwise poorly articulated insights even begin to make sense. A well-known Christian ethicist says it best:

> ...apart from the individual and corporate disciplines of the spiritual life of the Christian community, its sense of the Holy, of the transcendent withers; when its sense of the transcendent withers, the distinctive tone and quality of its moral activity is lost. Indeed, not only *how* it decides and acts is altered; the ends that it seeks to achieve and the limits on means that it imposes on itself might also be altered. *What* it does might also be altered.[4]

For the Christian, spirituality and morality have very much in common. To separate them unduly or to disregard the important ways in which they interact and influence each other renders a disservice to both and is harmful to the well-being of Christ's body, the Church, and the people it seeks to serve.

Spirituality and Moral Theology

A sobering truth now comes to the fore: in the history of theology, this delicate balance between the spiritual and moral spheres of life has not always been maintained with care; in some cases, their dissociation has been passively permitted and, at times, even actively pursued. To verify this claim, one need only to look at the variety of ways in which academic circles have tended in the past to define the discipline of moral theology itself, i.e., as that "part" of theology which studies human action inasmuch as it is subject to (1) virtue as a means to happiness, or (2) the contemplation of God as the ultimate end of human life, or

(3) law and obligation, or (4) duty imposed by reason, or (5) values contributing to the full realization of the human person.[5] Each of these "definitions" receives its special focus from a distinctive philosophical outlook. Respectively, these include the notions of peripatetic virtue, Thomistic teleology, Ockhamist nominalism, Kantian deontology, and personalist anthropocentrism. Each of them also puts forward a particular understanding of the relationship between the spiritual and moral life. These differences range anywhere from a relative integration based on varying combinations of the virtue-to-happiness constellation (as developed by Aristotle) and the nature/grace distinction (as traditionally held by St. Thomas) to a "coupling" or "stage" mentality (as encouraged by the nominalist and early Enlightenment distinction between moral and spiritual theology) to a complete dichotomy between the two (as promoted by Kantian deontology and its sharp distinction between pure and practical reason) to a tentative reintegration of the two (as evidenced with varying degrees of success in the general approach taken by the proponents of personalist ethics). The problem of the relationship between spirituality and morality becomes even more complex when one realizes that the actual emergence of moral theology as an academic discipline came relatively late in the history of the Church and that the sharp distinction between the spiritual and the moral as such surfaces in the tradition of Western Christianity precisely as a result of this move toward increased theological specialization.[6]

Father Paissy, an Orthodox monk and a minor character in Dostoyevsky's famous novel, makes a biting indictment of what specialization can do to theological knowledge. In a parting address to Alexei, the youngest of the three Karamazov brothers who is about leave monastery life and enter the secular world of nineteenth-century Russia, he shows his distaste for the way scientific method can easily despiritualize a person's perception of the sacred:

> "Always remember, young man…that secular science, having become a great force in the world, has, especially in the last century, investigated everything divine handed

down to us in the sacred books. After a ruthless analysis the scholars of this world have left nothing of what was held sacred before. But they have only investigated the parts and overlooked the whole, so much so that one cannot help being astonished at their blindness. And so the whole remains standing before their eyes as firm as ever and the gates of hell shall not prevail against it."[7]

These and similar sentiments are voiced down to the present day. More than one author has regretted the so-called "dissociation of sensibility" that method has effected in the world of theology since the time of the Enlightenment.[8] In its impulsive rush to model itself on the empirical sciences, theology, they claim, has lost touch with the nurturing role that it plays in the spiritual life of the believer. The unfortunate result of this gradual loss of contact has been an ever-widening gap between the theologian's rational reflections, his or her own interior sentiments, and those of the people he or she seeks to serve.

Related to this unhappy state of affairs are the invisible gaps that theological method opens between the insights of a sophisticated intellectual elite and those of popular religious culture. Unless they are careful, theologians can easily look down upon the popular masses and their "unenlightened" devotions; the latter, in turn, can feel threatened by what they do not understand and relegate the world of the theologian to the convenient waste bin of needless speculation. Finding and maintaining a delicate balance between sound theological reflection and authentic popular devotion is a challenge that must be taken up and dealt with by all believers, regardless of the number of academic degrees they have in their possession.

One of the many practical aims of spirituality is to help narrow and, in many cases, bridge these dangerous gaps and erstwhile cracks. To be distinguished from spiritual theology, the term assigned by the traditional theological nomenclature to the scientific study of the life of perfection (and which is often subdivided into the sub-disciplines of ascetical and mystical theology), spirituality is a "field-encompassing" discipline of relatively recent vintage, which focuses on how the whole of theology—in its various verbal, symbolic, bodily, and subliminal expressions—affects the living faith of the believer and the community to which he or she belongs.[9]

Of the variety of definitions that have been developed in recent years, one stands out as particularly perceptive. Spirituality is "…the way in which a person understands and lives within his or her historical context that aspect of his or her religion, philosophy or ethic that is viewed as the loftiest, the noblest, the most calculated to lead to the fullness of the ideal or perfection being sought."[10] In addition to its very broad, open character (thereby allowing it to be concretized in a variety of religious and even secular contexts), this definition has the additional strength of focusing on the highest aspirations of a person's particular belief-system. It is also flexible enough to allow for different dimensions of spirituality without falling into the dangerous pitfalls of theological equivocation. Three stand out in particular: (1) "the *real* or *existential* level," which focuses on the way a person or group brings to life in their own historical circumstances a specific religious or spiritual ideal; (2) "the *formulation of a teaching about this lived reality*"; and (3) "the *study* by scholars of the first and especially of the second levels of spirituality."[11] In this context, the scientific study of Christian spirituality is one step removed from a formalized spiritual teaching, which itself is one step removed from the lived or experiential level of spirituality.

Such an approach recognizes the intrinsic worth of the intellectual study of Christian spirituality as a whole (or even particular schools of spirituality), but not at the expense of formalized spiritual teaching and popular devotion. It presumes a continuity between all three levels and would be suspicious of anything that would try to separate experience from teaching and systematic reflection. When applied specifically to the relationship between Christian spirituality and morality, it will look upon moral theology as only one of many theological disciplines affecting the spiritual life of the Christian and Church community. As such, it will examine the moral tradition of the Church—in its whole and in its parts—from the perspective of how the believer is aided in realizing his or her highest aspirations.

Historiographical Considerations

A peculiar historiographical problem now comes to the fore. How does one speak of the historical relationship between spirituality and moral theology when both disciplines are relatively late arrivals on the theological scene of Western Christianity and arose as a response to particular philosophical and theological circumstances, many of which are no longer operative and have been long since forgotten? To project these disciplines (and the categories that they entail) onto an earlier period may hinder any attempt at finding what is truly distinctive of the particular historical period in question. To ask how believers of the early Church, for example, integrated their *spiritual* with their *moral* lives already implies that they understood the distinction between the two spheres and thus thought in categories at least vaguely similar to our own. Such a question fails to take into account the philosophical and theological mindset in which these early believers lived and exercised their faith. By asking it, we must wonder to what extent we are shaping the past to fit our own categories so that we can find our own reflection in it. Would it not be better to concern ourselves with the questions that these early believers themselves posed to the faith and the tradition of which they formed a part?

Given the fact that the disciplines of moral theology and spirituality have themselves undergone considerable development since their inception complicates the matter even further. Which definition of moral theology and which level of spirituality are we talking about when we search the past for relevant correlations to our present experience? What criteria will we use to distinguish a valid interaction from an illicit or an invalid one? How does method (a necessary tool in an essay of this sort) get out of its own way and allow the past to speak for itself and not to say only what we have preconditioned it to say?

All of these questions, when taken in conjunction with the fact that theology itself has undergone considerable change since its earliest apostolic proclamations and that the term itself replaced *sacra doctrina* as the prevalent term for the wide corpus of Christian belief and practice only late in the thirteenth century,[12] points out the enormity of the task ahead and highlights the care with which one must proceed. They also point to the impossibility of our leaving the present when we try to come to terms with the past. In this matter, the best we can hope for is to be sensitive to the problem, realize what we are doing, and try to enter into dialogue with the past rather than engaging in a senseless and generally useless monologue.

The Unfolding of a Tradition

We are now in a position to lay out in brief, cursory fashion how spirituality and morality have related to each other during the course of Christian history. The purpose of this short (and intentionally "limited") outline is not to exhaust the possibilities of their diverse interactions over time, but to provide a valuable touchstone or point of departure from which further reflection on the relationship between spirituality and morality in the Christian tradition can take place. At the very outset, however, it must be stated that the phrase I am using to describe this ongoing historical interplay already predisposes us to a certain way of looking at the rapport between spirituality and morality. To speak of "the unfolding of a tradition" implies a certain fullness of the tradition already existing *at the beginning*, if not in all its fine details, then at least in an unarticulated seminal form. The phrase, one might say, represents a type of theological discourse that structures an underlying (and, some would say, largely unverifiable) pattern of continuity into the very fabric of historical knowledge. If it provides us with a valuable heuristic device for drawing disparate material into a single synthetic whole (hence the reason for our employing it), we must also recognize that its conclusions are to be regarded as tentative and subject to further revisions, especially those that will highlight some of the discernible discontinuities present within the tradition.

1. With this opening qualification, let us begin with the supposition that the spirituality/morality discussion as it existed in early Aramaic and Hellenic Christian circles (i.e., before the destruction of the temple in 70 AD) centered on the nature of the relationship between the Mosaic Law and the New Covenant wrought by Jesus' death and resurrection. According to this scenario, the Aramaic-speaking Christians of Jerusalem (or Judaizers, as they are sometimes called) insisted on the binding nature of the more than 600 laws of the Torah on all adherents of the new faith, while the Greek-speaking Christians of Antioch (or Hellenizers) asserted that nobody could be justified by works of the law and thus opted for a relaxation of the requirements of the Law's numerous ceremonial and judicial precepts.[13] The point at issue here was not so much "law" versus "spirit," but to what extent was the Mosaic Law to be incorporated into a life lived according to the Spirit of Christ. Another way of viewing the tension would be to recognize that Jesus' gift to his followers was not that he added anything new to the Mosaic code, but that he identified the Golden Rule (Mt 7:12) as the means for determining what was essential in the law and what was not. From this perspective, the tension between the Judaizers and Hellenists in the earliest years of the Church stemmed more from a conflict in theologies or "spiritualities" of the law than (as we have often been led to believe) in a strong dichotomy between those wishing to adhere to the letter of the law and others wishing to be led by the promptings of the Spirit.

2. With the gradual eclipse of Jewish Christianity and the emergence of the Hellenizers as the predominant shapers of the nascent faith, tensions of a different sort developed out of the growing Gnostic tendencies of a number of early communities. The issue at stake here was not the applicability of the Mosaic Law but the legitimacy of a metaphysical dualism which pitted the world of spirit against an evil world of matter. The origins of this esoteric, mystical movement which swept the ancient world at roughly the same time as Christianity are uncertain (suggestions

range anywhere from Persian Zoroastrianism, to the ancient mystery cults of Mithras and Isis, to reactionary elements of a disillusioned Jewish fringe).[14] Whatever they were, it is clear that the diversity and malleability of Gnostic doctrine enabled it to penetrate and, in some cases, even flourish in a number of Christian communities of the later half of the first century (hence the term "Gnostic Christians"). The extreme difficulty in characterizing these beliefs extends also to their ethical practices, which could run the gamut from severe rigorism to nihilism and absolute moral laxism.[15] In the former case, ascetical practices were looked upon as a way in which the individual Gnostic could rise above the evils of the material world; in the latter, the divine spark existing within the believer was thought to guarantee salvation and thus permitted him or her to depart from traditional moral behavior. In either case, we generally find the use of a spiritual, other worldly outlook to justify or excuse specific types of moral behavior, something not unlike the way the spirituality-morality distinction would develop in later centuries.

3. If Christian orthodoxy met the Gnostic challenge by combining and having in place by the middle of the second century the structures of a strong monarchical episcopacy and the notion of an apostolic succession, it would meet still further challenges when facing the opposing heterodox extremes of Montanist spiritism and Arian rationalism. In neither case do we find a subtle separation of the spiritual and moral spheres, as was the tendency of certain Gnostic sects. Instead, we find the beginnings of a gradual dissociation of the spiritual life from the sphere of *sacra doctrina* itself. In the case of Montanism, this is evidenced in the strong emphasis given to the inspiration of the Holy Spirit in the prophetic utterances of its leaders, but with a lack of any firm authoritative structures for discerning the precise origin of that inspiration.[16] In Arianism, it is evidenced in what amounts to its "rationalist" portrayal of the Son as "the highest of all created creatures" and the repercussions it would have on our understanding of the economy of salvation.[17] From these moments on in its history, orthodox Christianity will be suspicious of an over-motivated and unreflective spiritualism, on the one hand, and an overt tendency to rationalize away the

mysteries of the faith, on the other. The balance between the two, while not always kept and, in many cases, miserably upset, will henceforth be looked upon as a goal to strive after and, with God's help, to achieve.

4. At the height of the patristic era, two powerful historical influences on orthodox Christianity would do much to help strike this balance for future centuries: the rise of the imperial model of Church in the fourth century and the Neoplatonic synthesis effected by such Christian authors as Augustine of Hippo (354–430) in the West and Pseudo-Dionysius (c. 500) in the East. In the case of the former, Christianity increasingly took on the trappings of the Constantinian court with its rigid hierarchical structures and its reliance on Roman law as an instrument for imposing order in a large, unwieldy empire.[18] In the latter case, Neoplatonism was stripped of its latent pagan propensities (e.g., emanationism; a tendency to denigrate the material world) and used as the philosophical basis for synthesizing and elucidating the Christian faith on its institutional, theological, and mystical levels.[19] So strong were the effects of these two historical influences that Christianity was able to deal effectively with further heterodox tendencies within its ranks (as in the case of Augustine's success in Pelagian and Donatist controversies) and adapt to changing political circumstances (as in the case of the papacy from the person of Gregory the Great filling a political vacuum when the empire fell in the West). Together, they were successful in effecting at least the idea, if not the reality, of a Christian synthesis on all levels of Church life (e.g., institutional, doctrinal, moral, mystical). The power of this idea captured the imagination of the medieval mind and, in many instances, makes its presence felt down to the present day.

5. The collapse of the Roman empire in the West inaugurated a gradual rift between Constantinople and Rome. The synthesis achieved during the patristic era continued unabated in the East for more than a thousand years and helped to insure the continuity of its spiritual, theological, and political traditions. In the West, however, it had a much more difficult time surviving and was preserved (although barely intact) largely through the efforts of Benedictine monasticism which, during centuries of fragmen-

tation, decline, and cultural isolation, provided one of the few stable institutions that could preserve the heritage of classical civilization and pass it along to future generations.[20] During these centuries, Augustine's Neoplatonic outlook attained unparalleled prominence in the West and left a deep impression (especially in monastic circles) on the mindset of medieval Christianity. His doctrine of original sin would be variously interpreted in subsequent generations and have profound repercussions on the spiritual and moral life of the Christian faithful, as would his emphasis on the spiritual senses of Scripture, the allegorical interpretation of the Scriptures, his strong emphasis on Divine Providence, and the efficacy of grace. Most significant was his theology of history, as set forth in *The City of God*, which succeeded in bringing together the Hebrew consciousness of God's activity in the world and the otherwise ahistorical tendencies of traditional Neoplatonic philosophy. For these and other reasons, the medieval West considered Augustine the Christian theologian par excellence.[21]

6. The ongoing interplay of ancient Greco-Roman civilization, Germanic culture, and the Christian religion gave the medieval West its distinctive shape and allowed for the possibility of further developments and cross-fertilizations in every sphere of life.[22] With the arrival of new technologies and social institutions that permitted the rise of a merchant class and the birth of a market economy, Western Europe was able by the middle of the eleventh century to emerge from centuries of feudal isolation and take on a larger, more confident role in its affairs with the rest of the known world. This expansive attitude made itself felt in the expansion of trade routes along the Mediterranean and in the interior regions of Europe and Asia. In the ecclesiastical sphere, it showed itself in the efforts of the Gregorian reformers, the growing centralization of papal powers, the launching of the first Crusades, and the rise of the mendicant orders.[23] Intellectually, Europe was ready for an influx of ideas that would help it to recast many of the insights of the Augustinian synthesis. It would find them in the thought of Aristotle, whose entire corpus would make its way into the Latin West during the course of the twelfth and thirteenth centuries, largely through the efforts of Muslim

translators from Spain and Sicily.[24] The rise of the scholastic method and the gradual shift from monastic to scholastic theology that took place during the course of the next century-and-a-half had a profound effect on the way the theological enterprise was conceived and carried out.[25] The stated purpose of theology was no longer the acquisition of wisdom, but the determination of the objective content of revelation. Allegoresis gave way to syllogistic reasoning; theological reflection gradually removed itself from the Biblical narratives; prayer became ancillary to theological reflection, rather than an integral part of the process of "faith seeking understanding."[26] If masters like Bonaventure and Aquinas managed to keep their balance and, in many cases, even improve on the synthesis started by Augustine, it was only a matter of time before the forces set in motion by the scholastic method would bring down a theological edifice that literally took centuries to build.

7. The figure who heralded this collapse was the early fourteenth-century Franciscan philosopher William of Ockham (1295–1349) who, armed with his famous principle of parsimony, questioned the existence of universals in the mind of God (as the Augustinian synthesis had held) and in particular things (as Thomas' Aristotelian synthesis had maintained). According to his Nominalist approach, only individual things existed and were subject to direct observation. What prior philosophies had identified as "forms" or "universals" were nothing but names invented by the human mind and then assigned to groups of particulars. Since particulars had nothing in common but their logical connections to the human mind, it was impossible to use them as a starting point for natural theology. Within this framework, the hierarchies of being and meaning, which both the Augustinian and the Thomistic syntheses had accepted (albeit in varying degrees), were no longer applicable. Human reason was incapable of coming to a natural knowledge of the divinity. God was known by Revelation alone and not bound to any particular manifestation of his power. An action was good solely because God willed it so. If so desired and provided there were no internal contradictions, God could have (and still can) set up an entirely different world with another moral code for humanity to

abide by.[27] From such ideas, it is easy to see how Ockham's inno-vations, when taken to their extremes, occasioned a great divide between human reason and Revelation, on the one hand, and, at least in theory, between God and the moral code, on the other. This divide also extended to the ecclesiastical, theological, and spiritual spheres. Ockham himself championed the theory of secular absolutism and wrote a number of treatises against the monarchical constitution of the Church. Theology lost its cohesiveness and gradually came to be thought of as a collection of highly specialized and only vaguely related sub-disciplines (e.g., dogmatic, moral, ascetical, mystical theology). Western mysticism lost its underlying intellectual justification and drifted to the periphery of theological reflection. In many ways, the spread of Nominalism cleared the way for many controversies of the Reformation: *sola Scriptura*, justification by faith, the lack of natural revelation—to name but a few. There is little doubt that Ockham's razor cut deeply into the traditional outlook of Medieval Christianity. Centuries later, the scars are still near the surface of the skin and visible to the eye.

8. *Numquam ponenda est pluralitas sine necessitate.*[28] If the nominalism of Ockham's *via moderna* was a major catalyst in the breakup of the medieval synthesis and loomed large behind the controversies that kindled the raging fires of the Reformation and, by way of reaction, the Counter Reformation,[29] it was not until the Age of the Enlightenment and Reason's so-called "coming of age" that its keen reductive and analytical tools were applied to the concept of Revelation itself. Ockham's focus on particulars prompted a more critical observation of the natural world and gave rise to the empirical method and the birth of modern science. Through their observations of natural phenomena and their search for "clear and distinct ideas," the philosopher-scientists of the Renaissance and early Enlightenment were able to discern specific patterns in the ways particulars behaved. During the course of the seventeenth and eighteenth centuries, it came to pass that God's direct intervention in the affairs of the world was no longer deemed necessary to explain the way particulars behaved. Miracles fell out of vogue, as did all other divine intrusions into the natural order, including that of Revelation.[30]

Once these ideas were tossed atop the junk pile of useless knowledge, the concept of God itself would increasingly move to the periphery of the West's cultural awareness. The Deists turned God into a distant and impersonal force that had left its mark in the observable order of the visible world. As Reason's confidence in the ability of scientific method to ascertain "the truth of things" continued to grow, even *that* notion came to be considered a useless anachronism. "Enlightened" rationalists observed that the laws of nature were not as universal as they had previously thought. A degree of uncertainty was perceived in the behavior of particulars. If reason could not reach beyond the phenomenal world and argue to the existence of God, and if the concept of God was not necessary for the advance of human knowledge, then why believe in God at all? Kant's radical separation of pure and practical reason moved the Western philosophical tradition on a long and harrowing turn toward the subjective.[31] A complete separation between the moral and the spiritual life had been effected. Humanity became the master of its own destiny and went busily about the construction of its own moral edifice— apart from any intrinsic reference to God.

9. By the latter half of the nineteenth century, Reason had nothing else to turn its razor-sharp edge on, but itself. Throughout the history of Western thought, it had been continually reinventing itself to fit an increasingly narrower understanding of its limits and criteria for its affirmations of truth. The movement from allegory to syllogism to induction in the hermeneutical tradition of the West reflects a parallel development in reason's own self-understanding that went from analogy to univocity to equivocation. The latter undermined the very notion of reason itself and became the instrument by which the masters of suspicion (i.e., Marx, Freud, and Nietzsche) pried open the cracks in Reason's foundation and broke through the walls of its otherwise impregnable fortress. In doing so, they heralded the end of the modern era and the beginning of what has come to be known as the postmodern world.[32] What is most peculiar about the systematic dismantling of Reason's rule over the last one hundred years is that it was achieved not by an all-out frontal assault (as in the Catholic condemnation of Modernism) or by

defying the reign of Reason's rule (as in Kierkegaard's existential embrace of the absurd), but from the inside working out. Deconstructionism was a logical outgrowth of the Enlightenment's fascination with the power of human reason. Amidst the debris of discontinuities and broken concepts it has left behind, a unique opportunity has arisen in the history of Western thought and culture, i.e., the retrieval of recently discounted elements of its rich philosophical and theological tradition and the possible reintegration of its moral and spiritual horizons. Whether the Church, or Western culture, or some indeterminate force outside of Western culture will take advantage of this opportunity remains yet to be seen.

Counter Discourse

The above outline, while by no means complete, offers a broad overview of what some like to refer to as the marriage, divorce, and remarriage of spirituality and morality in the history of Western Christianity. I recognize the inherent limitations of this (and, probably, any) attempt to provide the larger picture of this ongoing relationship. If preconceptions have colored my process of selection and have led me to focus more on some elements than others, I seek in the following theses to provide a helpful counter discourse that will point out areas in need of further study and directions that future research of the relationship between spirituality and morality might take.

Thesis One: The relationship between spirituality and morality in Western Christianity is partly a function of the way the changing perceptions of the way the concepts of God, the human person, and the world interact over time.[33] The presence of each of these elements is necessary in all mature theological reflection. The way they combine in any given historical period will tell us much about the kind of spirituality we can expect to find there as well as how that particular spirituality envisions its relationship to the moral life. Research into the ongoing historical relationship of these concepts will provide us with invaluable information that will launch us into still further areas concerning the integration of prayer and action.

Thesis Two: The relationship between spirituality and morality in Western Christianity is partly a function of the changing ways in which the Church has dealt with questions of orthodoxy and heterodoxy. The means and structures used by the Church to determine what comprises a legitimate expression of the faith have much to offer our understanding of the close interconnection between morality and life in the Spirit. On the one hand, adherence to the decalogue, the primary moral code of the Judeo-Christian tradition, has been used as an effective means of identifying heterodox spiritual traditions. On the other hand, many valuable insights into the spiritual life and the way it helps us to live the moral life have been neglected because of their association with intense denominational rivalries. Research into the history of the emergence of orthodoxy within the Christian tradition and its subsequent activity will do much to help us to integrate our understanding of the spiritual and moral life.

Thesis Three: The history of the relationship between spirituality and morality in Western Christianity is partly a function of changing understandings of the concept of rationality in the Western philosophical tradition.[34] The rapport between spirituality and morality is but a single facet of some much deeper questions, specifically those having to do with the relationship between philosophy and theology in Western civilization and with Western philosophy's own ongoing self-understanding. Further study of the historical relationship between Athens and Jerusalem and of those particular periods when the concept of rationality undergoes a noticeable shift will do much to deepen our understanding of our present concerns.

Thesis Four: The relationship between spirituality and morality in the tradition of Western Christianity is partly a function of changing notions of the nature and scope of theology itself. The movement in the history of theology from narrative and commentary to syllogism and synthesis, to induction, suspicion, deconstruction, and retrieval shows that *sacra doctrina* has experimented with (and often embraced) a variety of means to express the truths of the faith. The way spirituality relates to morality has much to do with the particular understanding of theology in vogue in a specific historical era. More research into the historical development of theology's own self-understanding will provide important information concerning the changing contours of this relationship down to the present.

Thesis Five: The relationship between spirituality and morality in the history of Western Christianity is partly a function of changes in perceptions concerning the rapport between nature and grace. A deeper knowledge of the historical contours of the origin and development of the nature/grace distinction will have an important effect on our understanding of the way life in the Spirit is related to the moral code. Research into how this distinction has, for example, influenced the way natural law has been variously construed and related to the concept of divine revelation will clarify much in the relationship between spirituality and morality. Natural law gives humanity access to the moral code apart from divine revelation. As such, it has the power to drive a wedge between morality and the spiritual life or to be a mediator between the two.

Thesis Six: The ongoing rapport between Christian spirituality and morality is partly a function of the changing idea of the Holy in the history of Western civilization. Christian spirituality and morality are here seen to be closely bound up with the changing contours of "the sacred" in the history of Western culture, especially in the requirements for sanctity and the control of those requirements by the institutional Church in the process of canonization. Further research into the changing ways in which the Holy is localized and given emphasis in the history of the Church (e.g, in the community, in the saint, in relics, in the clergy, in the consecrated host) will contribute to the discussion at hand. A study of the particular qualities or virtues that are emphasized throughout history as a requirement for sanctity (e.g., chastity, poverty, obedience, detachment, justice) will also do much to help us better understand the matter at hand.

Thesis Seven: The relationship between spirituality and morality in the history of Western Christianity is partly a function of changing attitudes toward the purpose and meaning of hierarchy. If for most of the Middle Ages hierarchy was thought of as a positive structure ordained by God for the correct ordering of every level of existence (e.g., the cosmos, society, the Church, the human person), its gradual separation from the structures of human cognition turned it into a culturally ambiguous concept which, depending on the context in which it was discussed, could arouse anything from strong affirmations to intense negative reactions. Research into the history or the changing notions of hierarchy in Western culture will help deepen our understanding of the connection between spirituality and morality, especially with regard to the various roles women played in coping with social and religious structures that were, for the most part, created and perpetuated by men.

Thesis Eight: The relationship between spirituality and morality in the history of Western Christianity is partly a function of changing notions of prayer and how it is integrated into the daily life of the ordinary believer. The way we pray has very much to do with the operative image of God offered to us by the culture in which we live. Methods of prayer will vary according to our understanding of how God looks upon us and interacts with us. A deeper understanding of the history of the forms of prayer and the way they were thought to impinge upon the life of the believer will give us a deeper understanding of the role of spirituality in the moral life.

Thesis Nine: The relationship between spirituality and morality in the history of Western Christianity is partly a function of ongoing developments in the Church's liturgical life, especially that of the Eucharist. The theological axiom *lex orandi, lex credendi* demonstrates the intimate role that the liturgy has played in the continuing formulation of the Church's doctrinal expressions. Strictly speaking, however, *lex credendi* extends to matters of both faith *and* morals. The liturgy maintains the integrity of the Church's moral life by instructing believers in the ways of Christ's love and by realizing the Christ event and the presence of the Spirit in the life of the community. Research focusing on changes in the Church's understanding of liturgical practice and its role in shaping the moral life of the community of believers will be a great help to discussion.

Thesis Ten: The relationship between spirituality and morality in the history of Western Christianity is partly a function of changing attitudes toward the nature and requirements of authentic mysticism. Comparisons between mystics of different historical epochs and the ways in which they relate to Church and society would bring valuable insights into the way the link between spirituality and morality is understood throughout the history of Western culture. Research focusing specifically on the changing rapport between mysticism and theology (e.g., fully integrated, peripherally related, completely detached) would also be of great value in our attempt to delineate more clearly the changing parameters of the discussion.

These theses identify just a few of the directions that future research might take regarding the historical relationship between spirituality and morality. They demonstrate the broad "field-encompassing" nature of such a study and raise our awareness of the complexity of the relationship and of some of the deep philosophical, theological, and cultural questions involved in the discussion. Taken both individually and as a whole, they provide valuable correctives to the tentative and summary sketch provided earlier. If nothing else, they hope to show that the unity, dissociation, and reintegration of spirituality and morality involves an interplay of a number of factors in a historical process that continues down to the present. All of these elements must be taken account in an adequate discussion of the unfolding of the tradition.

Conclusion

The historical considerations presented in this essay are an invaluable starting point for a mature, comprehensive discussion of the relationship between spirituality and morality. The contours of this relationship will vary according to our understanding of the terms themselves and how we, as historians, frame their ongoing interaction over time. They will also have much to do with the types of moral discourse we examine and the academic range we assign to the fields of spirituality and moral theology. Without this important historical context, we cannot expect to proceed very far in our investigation. With it, we at least have the assurance of setting out in the right direction with a relatively good idea of what we are looking for and why.

A fitting way to end our discussion will be to return briefly to Dostoyevsky's *The Brothers Karamazov*, this time to Ivan Karamazov's notorious tale of "The Grand Inquisitor." Set in sixteenth-century Seville during the time of the Inquisition, the story paints a horrifying picture of how morality can go awry once it is separated from its spiritual roots. Ivan, himself a die-hard cynic who believes everything is permitted and nothing barred, recounts an imaginary encounter between the cardinal Grand Inquisitor, an old man of nearly ninety who has con-demned thousands of heretics to death, and Jesus of Nazareth, a silent figure with a face of unlimited compassion, who has returned to the suffering world he once redeemed and who has himself been arrested and thrown into prison on charges of heresy. The Inquisitor, who lives by the rule of authority and power and who has already made up his mind to have Jesus burned at the stake, looks with disdain at his poorly clad prisoner and gives him a gloomy foreboding of things to come:

> "Do you know that ages will pass and mankind will proclaim in its wisdom and science that there is no crime and, therefore, no sin, but that there are only hungry people. 'Feed them first and then demand virtue of them!'—that is what they will inscribe on their banner which they will raise against you and which will destroy your temple."[35]

This prophecy comes from someone who knows nothing of prayer and whose moral life has become completely separated from its spiritual roots. If the Inquisitor's words in any way apply to our own times (as Dostoyevsky undoubtedly thought they did to his), we have to ask ourselves what kind of people have we become and what awful things are we ourselves doing in the name of goodness, truth, and right. The answer may surprise us.

It may be something very different from what we would like (or are even willing) to hear.

SUGGESTED READING

Aumann, Jordan. *Christian Spirituality in the Christian Tradition.* London: Sheed and Ward, 1985.

Bouyer, Louis, Jean Leclercq, François Vandenbroucke, and Louis Cognet. *A History of Christian Spirituality.* 3 Vols. Translated respectively by Mary P. Ryan, The Benedictines of Holme Eden Abbey, Carlisle, and Barbara Wall. Burns & Oates Ltd/ Desclée Co., Inc.: London/New York: 1963–69; reprint, New York: The Seabury Press, 1982.

Gallagher, John A. *Time Past, Time Future: An Historical Study of Catholic Theology.* New York/Mahwah, N.J.: Paulist Press, 1990.

Jones, Cheslyn, Geoffrey Wainwright, and Edward Yarnold, eds. *The Study of Spirituality.* Cambridge: University Press, 1986; second impression, 1992.

Leclercq, Jean. *The Love of Learning and the Desire for God.* 3d ed. Translated by Catharine Misrahi. New York: Fordham University Press, 1982.

Leech, Kenneth. *Experiencing God: Theology as Spirituality.* San Francisco: Harper and Row, 1985.

Louth, Andrew. *Discerning the Mystery: An Essay on the Nature of Theology.* Oxford: Clarendon Press, 1983.

Mahoney, John. *The Making of Moral Theology: A Study of the Roman Catholic Tradition.* Oxford: Clarendon Press, 1987.

_____. *Seeking the Spirit: Essays in Moral and Pastoral Theology.* London: Sheed and Ward, 1981.

Pinckaers, Servais (Th.). *Les sources de la morale chrétienne: sa méthode, son contenu, son histoire.* Études d'éthique chrétienne, no. 14. Fribourg, Suisse: Éditions Universitaires, 1985.

Principe, Walter H. "Toward Defining Spirituality." *Studies in Religion/Sciences religieuses* 12(1983): 127–41.

Schneiders, Sandra M. "Spirituality in the Academy." *Theological Studies* 50(1989): 676–97.

Sherry, Patrick. *Spirit, Saints and Immortality*. Albany: State University of New York Press, 1984.

Tabbernee, William. "Dissenting Spiritualities in History." *The Way* 28(1988): 138–48.

White, R.E.O. *The Changing Continuity of Christian Ethics*. Vol. 2, *The Insights of History*. Exeter: The Paternoster Press, 1981.

Chapter Two

The Dynamics of Conversion

BRIAN V. JOHNSTONE, C.SS.R.

The previous chapter has indicated that there is, in Roman Catholic life, a certain dissociation between spirituality and morality. There is a similar split between the scholarly disciplines of "spirituality" and "moral theology."[1] This chapter will be concerned more particularly with the latter problem. It will be proposed that a solution can be found by considering all theology, including spirituality and moral theology, as reflection on conversion. To develop this suggestion, an explanation of conversion is needed and this will be the subject of the following section.

Narratives of Conversion

When they think about conversion, many Christians will recall the narratives of the conversion of Peter (Mk 14:72), or Paul (Acts 22:3–11), or Augustine.[2] However, within the tradition, there have, of course, been other conversions and we might begin by considering two of them. Edith Stein was born in Breslau, Germany in 1891, a Prussian citizen and Jewish. She was a brilliant student and eventually became the assistant to Edmund Husserl at Freiburg-im-Breisgau. Her rigorous academic formation was shaped by his phenomenological method, the analysis of the phenomenon of consciousness. She earned an international reputation as a lecturer in Germany, Austria, and Switzerland.

On New Year's day 1922 she was baptized a Catholic and later she entered the Carmelite order. She was deported by the Nazis from the convent of Echt in 1942 and died in Auschwitz.

At 15, Edith decided that she did not believe in God. However, she gradually moved from atheism to a sympathy with Christianity. Since she was a profound thinker and highly educated, it might have been expected that theological and philosophical arguments would be important in her conversion. However, while these may have had a role, they were not decisive. There is evidence that she was no stranger to religious experience, perhaps including a certain mysticism.[3] One night in the summer of 1921 she was left alone in the house of a friend and happened to take up the autobiography of St. Teresa, *The Book of Her Life*. She read through the night, and as she closed the book she said to herself, "That is the truth."[4] As one commentator has written, "This is not the chance reading of a pious tale by a religious enthusiast. It is the disclosure of the divine within human history to one who was able to interpret it as such."[5] In the story of Edith Stein, it is religious conversion that is paramount. For others, the transformation was above all of a moral character, and this was the case for Bartolomé de Las Casas.

The conversion of Bartolomé de Las Casas (1474–1566) was a relatively unemotional, gradual process.[6] After his arrival in Hispaniola in 1502, Las Casas enjoyed life as an *encomendero*.[7] Although he exploited the slave labor of the Indians, he seems to have had no troubles in conscience. He was moved by the preaching of the Dominican friar Montesinos, who vehemently condemned these practices. However, Las Casas believed himself to be humane and paternal and saw no need to change either his ways or the system.[8] Even when he was refused sacramental absolution, specifically because of his neglect of his obligations to the Indians in his service, Las Casas was not convinced that he ought to give up his slaves.[9] Later, he acted as a chaplain during the "pacification" of Cuba, and was rewarded for this by being given an *encomienda*. Again, in good conscience, he took up his prosperous property.[10] In 1514, while preparing some sermons, he read the text of Sirach, concluding with 34:22: "He slays his neighbor who deprives him of his living: he sheds blood who denies the laborer his wages." This time his conscience was aroused.[11] The moral insight that he gained was further illuminated by religious faith, or, we might say, his moral conversion was taken up into a religious conversion. He came to see Indians as children of God, and then arrived at the more profound insight that, in the suffering Indians, Christ himself was present.[12] He gave up his *encomienda* and began to speak out against the colonists' exploitation of the Indians. Las Casas spent the rest of his life battling and writing on behalf of the rights of the Indians.[13] In doing so, he made a notable contribution to the development of the doctrine of rights, liberty, and cultural progress,[14] and anticipated many of the concerns of liberation theology.[15]

Michael Buckley has recently drawn attention to the extraordinary fact that so much Catholic theology, because of the divorce between spirituality and theology, has failed to appreciate the relevance of such experiences. He notes, moreover, that "...theology neither has nor has striven to forge the intellectual devices to probe in these concrete experiences the warrant they present for the reality of God and make them available for so universal a discipline."[16] We could add that moral theology has been similarly deficient in failing to explore such experiences for what they might tell us about Christian values and how they actually transform human lives. This chapter offers some tentative steps toward the development of the interpretative devices that are needed if we are to reach a fruitful understanding of such experiences.

The Meaning of Conversion

Conversion is a profound and ultimately mysterious experience and no explanation can be adequate. When asked about her own conversion, Edith Stein is reported to have replied, "That is my secret."[17] There have, however, been many studies of conversion,[18] and it is possible to offer some interpretations of this complex human reality. Bernard Lonergan described conversion as "...an ongoing process, concrete and dynamic, personal, communal and historical."[19] Lonergan uses the terms "concrete and dynamic" to indicate actual historical events, characterized by movement, change and conflict.[20] In particular, he stresses the distinction between abstract logic and the "proofs" it produces, and the concrete reality of conversion.[21] The connections grasped in conversion have a compelling quality beyond anything that abstract logic can produce. The distinction between the concrete and the abstract was, of course, a key point in John Henry Newman's distinction between notional and real assent. Conversions are concrete, and yield real assent.[22]

The analysis of conversion that follows takes the other points in Lonergan's description as a schema. Particular attention will be given to moral conversion, but other dimensions will also be included.

Personal

Lonergan explains religious conversion as an experience of being in love with God without restriction.[23] This dynamic state is not the product of our human efforts, but of grace. Indeed, it can be said that it is divine grace operating in us.[24] Some of Edith Stein's writings, even before her explicit conversion to Catholicism, reflect an awareness of a resting in God, of a life-giving power that is not one's own that must surely indicate religious conversion.[25] Again, for Lonergan, moral conversion is self-transcendence, in which the criterion of one's decision is changed from self-satisfaction to values.[26] He acknowledges that there will be resistance to such a conversion, and attributes this to bias.[27] There seems to be built into the human will a powerful opposition to any such transcendence. The discovery of the will and its resistance was a most important factor in the historical Christian tradition and had a great significance for both moral theology and spirituality.

There has been much discussion over recent decades as to whether there is or is not a specifically Christian ethic.[28] This debate has usually been about the content of the Christian ethic, that is, its precepts and prohibitions, and its motivation. However, there is a more profound level at which the Christian ethic is indeed specifically different from others. Greek ethics was based on a theory of nature, which supposed that everyone is moved by a love for the good. According to this view, we can turn away from the good, either because we make a mistake as to where it is to be found, or because of poor education and bad habits. However, for Augustine, these were not the real problems. For him there was a central crisis in human nature, the perversity of the will.[29] He records his intense experience of this in the pages of the *Confessions* which precede the account of his conversion. There he writes of "the controversy raging in my heart, a controversy about myself against myself."[30] He found illumination in the text of Paul's letter to the Romans: "My inner self agrees with the law of God, but I see in my body's members another law at war with the law of my mind..." (Rom 7:22–23).[31] While he found some truth in the Platonists, he now saw that they knew nothing of the grace which heals the will, of the humble heart, or of the tears of confession. What emerges from Paul and Augustine is an ethic which is profoundly different from the warrior ethic of the earlier Greeks, or the self-mastery of Plato, or the honor ethic of later Europe, or the contemporary ethics of "taking care of yourself" or of autonomous self-expression. It is an ethic of transformation of the will, made possible by grace, and manifested in conversion. St. Thomas Aquinas himself, while accepting the Greek Aristotelian view that everyone is moved by love for the good, recognizes an ineradicable disobedience in the will that can be healed only by grace.[32] A fundamental feature of conversion, as this tradition has presented it, is the transformation of the will, which includes the experience, both of the perverse resistance of the will, and of healing grace, freely given by God.

In the theological tradition, conversion has been interpreted as an encounter between divine and human freedom. This was not an easy matter to explain and the search for an adequate account generated many difficult questions. Is conversion something which the free woman or man achieves alone, by personal effort? Or is it a pure gift which is given to a radically unfree being, who becomes free only through the gift? Is it blind and irrational, a seizure of the person by mysterious forces which shut out understanding and free choice? Or does it touch the person by engaging thought and respecting liberty? For the Catholic tradition, conversion is pure gift, but one which does not negate the integrity of the human intellect and will. This means that, in the process of conversion, God's grace is primary and essential, but persons cooperate with grace, as intelligent and free beings.[33]

The relationship of divine initiative and human cooperation is explained in the classic treatment of conversion by St. Thomas Aquinas. He describes the interplay of the two in a delicate symphony, where the divine initiative is always respected, but human cooperation is never denied.

> The first principle of such acts is God's operation converting the heart...The second act is a movement of faith. The third is a movement of servile fear, by which a person is drawn away from sin by fear of punishment. The fourth is a movement of hope, by which one makes a purpose of amendment, in the hope of obtaining pardon. The fifth is a movement of charity whereby sin itself is displeasing in itself, and not in view of punishment. The sixth act is a movement of filial fear whereby a person, out of reverence for God, voluntarily offers amendment to God.[34]

Communal

Here attention is directed to the social dimension of conversion. This includes aspects which, according to some critics, Lonergan did not take sufficiently into account.[35] Liberation theologians, and Gustavo Gutiérrez in particular, have drawn our attention to the social, critical dimension of conversion. Gutiérrez emphasizes that "Conversion means a radical transformation of ourselves; it means thinking, feeling and living as Christ—present in exploited and alienated persons."[36] Thus, the transformation cannot be a purely interior phenomenon; the energy it generates radiates out and modifies social structures. For Gutiérrez, "To be converted is to commit oneself to the process of the liberation of the poor and oppressed."[37] Clearly, this was the form taken by Las Casas' conversion.

Contemporary theology expresses the social dimension of sin, and also implicitly of conversion, when it speaks of the "structures of sin."[38] Such language has now become part of the official teaching of the Church. Pope John Paul II has written of

> ...specific structures of sin which impede the full realization of those who are in any way oppressed by them. To destroy such structures and replace them with more authentic forms of living in community is a task which demands courage and patience.[39]

Conversion, then, includes action aiming at this kind of social transformation. Indeed, it extends even beyond this to include the whole human environment or "human ecology."[40] Thus, the person, changed by conversion, becomes a source of transforming energy for society and the world.

Historical

The historical dimension of conversion appears in the cultural traditions of communities. Conversions can only be understood when they are situated in the living tradition of a community. In this context, we could recall what Charles Taylor has said about the importance of "articulation."[41] When something has been present in the tradition in the language of the Bible and devotion, it is a possibility for those who inhabit the tradition. I would suggest that we might also say that conversion exists for us as a possibility because it has been talked about in the narratives of Peter, Paul, Augustine, Teresa, Edith Stein, and the many others which our tradition includes. These narratives include both the personal stories and the accounts of the impact of those stories on the tradition, an impact which often produces transformations in the tradition itself.

To explain this further, we can invoke the notion of "narrative" or "dramatic narrative" as this is used by some contemporary authors.[42] Narrative, in this sense, does not mean any kind of story; rather it is a way of displaying transformations and connecting sequences in belief and attitude, in the lives of persons and in the traditions of communities. Such a narrative has an order or rational structure that is revealed in the narrative and can be discovered by reflection. In other words, when we study these stories of how people themselves changed, and how they changed their traditions, we see that they have laid down paths which make sense, which lead somewhere and which can be followed by others, including ourselves. Narratives of transformation constitute a significant part of the tradition of the historical community that is the Church.

The German theologian Josef Pieper has suggested that tradition may also, in some way, include certain convictions of which we are normally not conscious, but which manifest their presence under certain conditions. These relate to salvation, condemnation, guilt, and happiness. They are not open to rational proof, and yet we orient our lives according to them, and feel at odds with ourselves when we seek to go against them.[43] It seems plausible to suggest that the mysterious dynamisms which lead to conversion may include, together with explicit narratives, such unconscious elements. William James, the Harvard philosopher, writing in the early years of the century, also reflected on this possibility. He proposed that in the process of conversion there is a breaking-in to the conscious mind of connections that had long been forming in the unconscious.[44]

The grasping of new connections was clearly a major element in the conversions we have examined earlier, and would seem to be an essential aspect of all conversions. Further, these sequences of ideas and feelings have a cohesive force which cannot be accounted for only by the logical links between ideas. This cohesion may be explained by suggesting that in the conversion process, the narrative which triggers the transformation meshes with powerful unconscious forces, and the new connections which result share something of this power.

However, we cannot account for the profound and enduring energy of genuine conversions in exclusively psychological terms. To explain it, we need to probe deeper and explore how personal freedom is involved. Here it will be helpful to return to the story of Edith Stein. What seems to have been fundamental to her conversion was an absolute commitment to truth.[45] Such a commitment would require that at some time in her life, she achieved a fundamental option or conversion to truth as an absolute value.[46] This in turn would presuppose the working of grace, the free gift which makes possible such a fundamental orientation of freedom. Through the mediation of the "external grace" of St. Teresa's narrative, Edith saw the connection between her fundamental commitment to truth and the historic, Catholic tradition. We may note that it was not a structured, logical argument, but a narrative that enabled her to make the connection. As Newman wrote, what brings about this kind of change is not argument, but "...a message, a history, or a vision."[47] Here, therefore, there is a coming together of a narrative, borne by the tradition, an interior orientation of freedom at the deepest level, something of which Edith Stein was aware,[48] and a new pattern of connections that found expression in her own narrative. These complex factors would seem to be the basis for the extraordinary cohesion and unwavering consistency of her subsequent life. It is not difficult to imagine that somewhere, someone else has read her story through the night and, at dawn, been led to affirm, "That is the truth."

An Ongoing Process

There is a basic conversion which initiates the process of transformation. The suggestion has already been noted that Edith Stein must have made such a basic conversion to the value of truth. But the Christian life is a process of continual conversion, which is a radiation of the energy of that first event into all the faculties and attitudes of the person. This process leads toward the transformation and unification of our whole being by divine love.[49] In its social and historical aspects, conversion is also an ongoing process. Thus, we have seen how a personal conversion, transposed into narrative and embodied in tradition, can make possible other conversions, which themselves enter into the tradition.

In the context of this ongoing process, we can appreciate the role of formal theological discourse. In the analysis of conversion thus far, little has been said about the role of theological argument. Does it have a place? From the example of the two persons we have discussed, it is abundantly clear that it does. Las Casas, in the course of his long defense of the Indians, was engaged in many theological debates. It is now recognized that he contributed significantly to the development of theology in the Catholic tradition.[50] Although she was not indifferent to the kind of questions which concerned Las Casas,[51] Edith Stein's intellectual work was directed more to the enrichment and transformation of the world of culture. Besides her own philosophical and theological writings, she published translations of St. Thomas Aquinas' work *On Truth*[52] and translations of Newman.[53] We might say that the complex philosophical and theological reflections that they developed flowed from their conversion and served to communicate the power of those conversions into the social and cultural spheres. Their thought became embodied in the public world of texts, articulating the dynamism of conversion and so making it available to others.

"Extraordinary" Conversions and "Ordinary" Conversions

Of course, for many Christians, and certainly for Catholics, dramatic accounts of conversion are something to read and wonder about, rather than a description of the kind of experiences they might have had or anticipate having in their lives. However, this should not lead us to think that real conversion is not part of the normal Christian life. Karl Rahner noted that the occurrence of conversion as a central event in the history of one's personal salvation is often masked in the experience of Catholics.[54] Baptism is usually administered to infants, First Communion occurs in childhood; the Sacrament of Reconciliation is experienced most often as a repeated setting right of moral fault, rather than an intense new birth.

Even if some Christians do not express conversion in the forms we encounter in reading Augustine, this does not mean that the reality of conversion is absent in their lives. The theologians, including Rahner himself, who developed the notion of the "fundamental option" have suggested that the acts which we perform on the level of everyday consciousness are the expressions of something more fundamental, an orientation of our freedom by which we direct our whole lives to God. Similarly, it could be suggested that some of the significant changes that we make in our everyday moral and spiritual lives are the manifestations of a more fundamental transformation or conversion, which never attains the dramatic form of the classic narratives of conversion, but which is nonetheless real.

Theology as Reflection on Conversion

The experience of conversion is the concrete, historical locus, where the divine freedom engages human freedom and brings about real change. That change is displayed in personal narratives, embodied in the narratives of the tradition, and explicated in subsequent argument. For theology, as the study of the ways of God in regard to humanity, conversion is clearly an appropriate place to begin. This does not mean that we bypass revelation as the source of theological reflection; it simply means that we focus on the concrete, transforming effects of revelation in history.

For Bernard Lonergan, theology is reflection on conversion.[55] Conversion is fundamental to religion. Theology, therefore, as reflection on religion has its foundation in conversion. This would mean that the focus of theology will be directed at the transforming or converting subject, who is behind all statements about religion.[56] In other words, the fundamental reality with which theology is concerned is the personal transformation which God brings about in Edith Stein, Bartolomé de Las Casas, and those many others who are converted, with or without a dramatic story. Lonergan's own explanation of how this works out is rather cryptic and calls for some further reflection.[57]

According to Lonergan, conversion transforms the concrete individual, to make that individual capable of grasping both principles and conclusions.[58] When we set out to explain something, we do so by establishing connections, showing that conclusions follow from principles. However, it is a common experience that we may have such an explanation before us, but not be drawn to assent to it. On the other hand, sometimes we may be convinced of a position, but only later come to justify that position by explaining it in terms of conclusions from principles. In particular, unless we have been transformed by moral conversion, a moral argument remains for us an abstract link up between propositions, with no power to generate assent and shape our choices.

Apparently the arguments of the preacher and those of the confessor who refused him absolution remained abstractions as far as Las Casas was concerned. Even the Scriptures, in his previous reading of them, had not been able to touch him. It seems that it was only when he was morally converted that such arguments made sense or "came together." Similarly, it would appear that it was on the basis of a prior intellectual and moral conversion that Edith Stein was able to recognize the truth in St. Teresa's story and, through that, see the truth in the Catholic tradition. We do not have access to the interior conversions of such persons, but we can study the narratives of that process and of their subsequent living out of their conversion. To say that theology should reflect on conversion is to say that it should begin not with abstract doctrines, but with the concrete, historical transformations of persons and communities, which God's free gift produces, as displayed in narratives.[59]

How might theology be done in this way? In the first place, it would give an important place to the analysis of the conversions and the lives of "the saints."[60] Theology would thus begin with the analysis of experience. This is, of course, an ambiguous word and must be used with care.[61] Here, it refers to experiences of conversion and, in particular, to those which are recorded in the narratives that have been acknowledged in the tradition and become, in a sense, "classics."[62] Examples are the *Life* of St. Teresa or, in the area of moral theology, the works of Las Casas.

Secondly, it would explore the meaning of that experience. Thus, it would investigate the traditions in which the narratives have their place and meaning, and analyze how persons concerned transformed the tradition. For example, Gustavo Gutiérrez has done this recently in his work on Las Casas.[63] When Las Casas pleads the case of the poor of the Indies, he is not developing abstract theories of justice; he is thinking of people whom he had personally seen massacred.[64] But he does develop theories of justice, since these are necessary to plead the cause of the Indians and bring about the legal and political changes which are needed. When we study these theories within the narrative, we can sense reverberations of the original experience that inspired them, and at the same time appreciate the force of the arguments they present. The concreteness of the experience behind the argument gives the argument a compelling quality that can induce in us an assent which is not merely abstract and notional but real.

A third task would be the development of criteria for judging the truth of experiences, narratives, and traditions. Particular narratives have meaning in traditions and must be judged true by the criteria of the tradition. The goal of the Christian tradition as a whole is to bring persons into a transforming relationship with God in Jesus Christ. This then constitutes its criterion of truth. A narrative, a more particular tradition, or a transformation of the tradition, will be true insofar as it leads persons in this direction. A fourth task would be to draw out the normative implications of conversion. For example, a genuine conversion requires a person to identify with the disadvantaged and, where oppressive social structures are present, to work to change them.

The Separation of Spirituality from Moral Theology

The previous chapter has described the history of the dissociation between spirituality and moral theology and the unfortunate consequences which followed.[65] Here we will offer a possible solution to the problem. Both spirituality and moral theology are disciplines with specific interests and goals. As has been explained in that earlier chapter,[66] "spirituality" considers the whole of theology and studies how it affects the believer's life of faith in community. Moral theology seeks to discover, in the light of revelation, the kind of persons Christians are called to become and the norms which should guide their lives. Moral theology, therefore, is a more specific field within the broader "field-encompassing" range of spirituality. There is, therefore, a distinction between the two.

However, as has been argued in this chapter, all theological reflection should begin with reflecting on concrete, historical conversions. In such conversions, and in the narratives which express them, faith and action, the spiritual and the moral, are fused in a complex union. Therefore, the disciplines of spirituality and moral theology have, as their basic subject matter, a unified experience. It has also been argued that subsequent theological reflection and analysis serve the purpose of analyzing, explaining the meaning of, validating, and drawing out the normative implications of conversion. The point of all this is to make those narratives more readily available in the tradition, as the foundation for further conversions. Thus, spirituality and moral theology have a common goal. Both are ultimately directed to bringing persons into a transforming relationship with God in Jesus Christ. Thus the disciplines are one in their starting point and one in their goal. They have, therefore, a fundamental unity.

The next step is to explain how spirituality and moral theology fulfill their distinct functions within their fundamental unity. Edith Stein, whose name in religion was Sister Teresa Benedicta of the Cross, had a profound spiritual sense of a call to suffer with Christ and thereby to participate in his redeeming work.[67] On August 2, 1942 in reprisal for a letter of the Dutch Bishops denouncing the persecution of the Jews, all "non-Aryan" Catholics in Holland were arrested, including Sister Benedicta.[68] She was taken away to Auschwitz. The last report of her comes from a soldier who saw her in the appalling conditions of the freight train which took her there.[69] No doubt, her spiritual vision enabled her to face this brutal degradation and the death to which it was leading and to see it all as ultimately redemptive. Her vision enabled her to endure in a way that transparently manifested sanctity.[70]

However, that vision did not necessarily provide answers to moral questions. As the possibility of deportation by the Nazis grew more threatening, Edith had to face some moral choices. She was urged to leave her convent and hide in another, as many other "non-Aryans" had done. But she refused to do something "illegal."[71] One of her arguments was that this could have very bad consequences for her present convent. This is clearly a prudent and selfless consideration. Her second argument was that Protestants in Germany believed that Catholics were "flexible" with the truth and she did not want to add to this bad reputation. If she could not be saved with the consent of the political administration, she would accept her fate.[72] At least to an outsider who knows little of the circumstances, this argument must seem very strange. The implied acceptance of the legitimacy of the Nazi administration, in particular, is hard to accept.

Las Casas' vision enabled him to see in the Indian the suffering Christ. That vision did not provide answers to the difficult moral questions concerning slavery, land rights, and the justification of war, which he worked on for years. But the vision does explain why he pursued those questions with tireless energy for decades, and why he could not be content with abstract theorizing, but carried his conclusions into action. Of course, Las Casas himself was wrong at times and notoriously so in his support of black slavery in the Indies. He himself somewhat belatedly, in 1547, found out what was really going on, changed his position and denounced all slavery, of Indians or blacks.[73] Prior to this, he accepted the prevailing view which justified some slavery.

Spirituality and morality come together in the original experience of conversion and come together in the concrete choices people make. However, in between there is a necessary place for moral theological reflection and critique. A spiritual vision can coexist in an individual's mind with moral suppositions that are wrong. We could cite as examples Edith Stein's apparent assumption of the legitimacy of the Nazi regime and Las Casas' acceptance of slavery. The relationship between the two is, therefore, complex and conditioned by historical circumstances. However, it is equally clear that the separation of spirituality and moral theology is a mistake. A profoundly authentic spiritual vision does not necessarily lead to correct moral theological conclusions. On the other hand, right moral conclusions can be reached without immediate dependence on a particular spiritual vision. But both must be present in a genuine, living tradition. A tradition without a spiritual vision of God and of union with God as the goal of life does not know where it is going and is mute in the face of profound evil and death. A tradition without moral theological reflection, critique, and argument cannot deal adequately with particular historical realities.

SUGGESTED READING

Augustine of Hippo. *The Confessions of St. Augustine*. Translated by F. J. Sheed. London/New York: Sheed and Ward, 1944.

Conn, Walter. *Christian Conversion: A Developmental Interpretation of Autonomy and Surrender*. New York: Paulist Press, 1986.

————, ed. *Conversion: Perspectives on Personal and Social Transformation*. Staten Island, N.Y.: Alba House, 1978.

Gaventa, Beverly Roberts. *From Darkness to Light: Aspects of Conversion in the New Testament*. Philadelphia: Fortress Press, 1986.

Gutiérrez, Gustavo. *Las Casas: In Search of the Poor in Jesus Christ*. Maryknoll, N.Y.: Orbis, 1993.

Happel, Stephen and James J. Walter. *Conversion and Discipleship: A Christian Foundation for Ethics and Doctrine*. Philadelphia: Fortress Press, 1986.

James, William. *The Varieties of Religious Experience*. New York: Macmillan, 1967.

Kittle, G. and G. Friedrich, eds. *Theological Dictionary of the New Testament*. Grand Rapids: Eerdmans, 1964–76. S. v. "Metanoia."

Nock, Arthur D. *Conversion. The Old and the New in Religion from Alexander the Great to Augustine of Hippo*. Oxford: Oxford University Press, 1961.

Pasquier, Jacques. "Experience and Conversion." *The Way* 17(1977): 114–22.

Rahner, Karl, ed. *Encyclopedia of Theology: The Concise Sacramentum Mundi.* New York: The Seabury Press, 1975. S. v. "Conversion," by Karl Rahner.

Rende, Michael L. *Lonergan on Conversion: The Development of a Notion.* Lanham, Md.: University Press of America, 1991.

Stein, Edith. *Life in a Jewish Family: 1891–1916: Her Unfinished Autobiographical Account.* Translated by Josephine Koepel. Washington, D.C.: ICS Publications, 1986.

Chapter Three

A Sense of Vocation

LYNDA ROBITAILLE

Have the teacher of spirituality and the teacher of moral theology anything in common? Should they approach their disciplines in a similar manner? Is the content of what they teach in any way related? At first glance, one may be tempted to answer "No" to such simply-stated but nonetheless intriguing and complex questions. Further reflection, however, shows that the two professions actually share a great deal in common. Ideally, the teachers of these subjects seek to communicate not only an academic discipline, but also a way of life. If their classes are nothing more than mere intellectual exercises, then what they achieve will fall far short of the commonly accepted goals and purposes of effective theological education. The teachers of these disciplines help their students to make considered decisions about their lives with the help of prayer and a mature knowledge of the faith which they profess. They, one might say, are the vehicles through whom the student comes to both an intellectual and a faith understanding of his or her relationship with God and the world.

Because of the importance of the teacher in the learning process, those who teach spirituality or moral theology should have a profound understanding of their own vocations. As teachers of an academic discipline, they need an intellectual mastery of their fields; as devoted Christians, they require a strong, living faith. An intellectual knowledge of spirituality or moral theology that is not nourished by a strong faith will be an ineffectual vehicle of the message being taught. If a teacher is not presenting an approach to spirituality or moral theology that is both intellectual and lived, the message will be weakened. It may even harm the student, who hears an intellectual or academic explanation of the history and meaning of these disciplines, but who does not learn how to relate these disciplines to life. The same is true of the teacher who presents only a practical approach to spirituality or moral theology, without grounding those practical guidelines in their immediate theological and historical context. Those who receive such training will not have all the proper tools for living an authentic Christian life.

In this chapter, I will consider how moral theology and spirituality are disciplines that need to be taught effectively for the good of the students and for the life of the Church. Since the teacher plays a crucial role in the learning and growth processes, he or she has a responsibility not only to know a particular academic field, but also to be a true disciple of Christ. Teaching spirituality or moral theology is the responsibility and privilege of those whom God has called to grow closer to him through this work and way of life.

Spirituality and Moral Theology: Theological Disciplines

Theology is a sacred science which has evolved into a number of different specializations (e.g., biblical theology, dogmatic theology, moral theology, canon law, spirituality, etc.). What links these disciplines together is the stated purpose of theology itself: to study all things under the light of God's revelation. Even though these disciplines have become more and more specialized in time, this single purpose unites them and makes them different aspects of the same theological enterprise.[1]

A consequence of this tendency toward increased specialization was that the various disciplines of theology gradually became more and more separated from one another and sometimes even from life itself. Some branches of theology became a purely academic pursuit that had little in common with the everyday faith experience of Christians. At the same time, spirituality and morality—being more praxis oriented—were concerned with the experience of people and seemed to have little to do with an academic and intellectual understanding of the Church and its beliefs.[2]

In the last few centuries, spirituality and moral theology have been treated separately both from each other and from the more theoretical theological disciplines. The teacher's own spiritual or moral life seemed to have little bearing on his or her teaching. In practice, spirituality was often taught in isolation from the other specializations. The practical implications of theology were separated more and more from its academic understanding, even to the point that the spirituality of the teacher was considered a separate rather than an integral element of who he or she was as a person and a Christian. As one author notes: "Even personally devout theological educators fail to relate their teaching and research to spirituality."[3]

Moral theology has been marginalized in a similar way from the more abstract theological disciplines:

> What is moral theology about if not the conduct, the right conduct, the orthopraxis of Christians? The relatively late distinction between dogmatic or doctrinal theology and moral theology as it began to prevail from the seventeenth century was based on a distinction between the study of revelation as truth or truths to be believed by Christians and a study of the practical or moral demands which they had to fulfill.[4]

It is now recognized that the moral behavior of a Christian consists of more than following the rules. The mature Christian must learn what the moral principles are, from where they come, and how they are to be interpreted. This interpretation entails a balance of the intellectual and the spiritual: the student must integrate the history of the ideas into his or her own spiritual life and become a disciple of Christ, learning to follow him in his or her own life, in daily decisions and prayer. Discipleship and spirituality need to be taught in light of Scripture, the history of the Church, and the world we live in. Spirituality, moral thinking, and ethical decision-making must be integrated into an academic curriculum so that they complement one another.[5]

Teachers of spirituality and moral theology are, by definition, teachers of theology. To consider their vocation under this broader category would not be forcing upon them an artificial constraint. Both spirituality and moral theology are specializations within the larger discipline of theology.[6] Although they employ different ways of approaching the revelation of God, both offer practical understandings of how to live a Christian life in behavior and in prayer. These insights should be taught in similar ways to achieve the common end: to give the students a strong understanding of their faith, based on revelation and tradition, as well as a good basis for interpreting the tradition, relating it to their own lives, and adjusting to the signs of the times. In other words, the primary goal of teaching these disciplines is to enable the student to grow into a mature, thinking, articulate Christian.

One of the great difficulties in teaching theology is finding (and then maintaining) the right balance between the academic discipline and the living out of its practical implications. Both aspects must be taught: the student must learn not only the rich traditions of the Church, but also how to make moral choices and to build a spiritual relationship with God. The emphasis must be on attaining a fine, delicate balance: to learn the riches of the tradition of the Church, and to put that tradition into practice. As one author notes:

> Practical theology begins with our lived experience and action in the world...practical theology's foundational question is, 'what is God's word and will in this particular place, time, and circumstance?' With praxis at its heart it consciously breaks with the theory-to-practice paradigm of classical theology and involves collaborating with God in 'world making' in light of Gospel values.[7]

What must be avoided is a complete separation of the lived Christian experience from one's intellectual knowledge of theology. Teachers of theology must avoid "the unreflective transmission of doctrine, the rote learning."[8] These will not help the student to internalize and integrate the knowledge into his or her everyday life. What must be avoided in the specific areas of moral theology and spirituality is too much stress on practice, and not enough emphasis on theory, ideas, and history. The student should be able to learn both the practical and the academic and be able to integrate the two in his or her life. This is graphically described by one author who illustrates the point by citing an extreme:

> Why is it that the term 'prayer' elicits from most of us an immediate association with 'spirituality' while few even of those who make their living by teaching theology associate spirituality with...thought?[9]

The Goal of Teaching Theology

How are the intellectual understanding and the everyday practice of one's faith bound together? They are bound together as the dual goal of the discipline of teaching of theology. If a theology professor teaches only one or the other aspect—in other words, if the students have a good intellectual understanding of their faith, but no understanding of how to live it, or vice versa — then he or she has fallen short of the stated goals of theological education. An intellectual understanding of theology can promote our faith and strengthen it. Through the study of theology, we reflect on the Christian tradition and its meaning for our lives; we learn how the academic theories or concepts are actually lived out in our personal lives and in the Christian community. This integration of the theoretical and the practical can only come from the teacher, the one who is called to work for the intellectual and spiritual formation of the students.[10] The challenge is to bring the students to an integration of the history and intellectual knowledge of theology, together with the practice of and growth in faith. To have such a goal leads to the question of the purpose of a theological education. Is the purpose of a theological education to "form" students into mature Christians? Or should educators merely address the academic matter in the curriculum and allow the formative matter to take care of itself, in more spiritually or morally-oriented environments? It seems that one cannot separate the two and that if the two were separated, the students would suffer. The education that they would receive would not be truly theological because it would not be a balanced presentation of the living faith of the Church.

This can only become clear when one outlines what the point of a theological education is. What do we want from these students? An ability to argue intellectually and dispassionately about points of doctrine or law or Scripture? Or an ability to understand those arguments, but also to relate them to their own lives and the lives of Christians around them? One religious educator describes it this way:

> Few would disagree with the proposal that a theological education involves much more than the transmission of information about the Bible, the history of the Church, the development of religious ideas, the modes and patterns of ethical thoughts and the like. Few would agree that the critical aspects of theological education involve only logical analysis of theological or ethical arguments, historical explanations of important events and persons in the history of the Church, and the like...theological study is not merely the storage of information or the training in professional techniques; it involves the shaping of the life outlook of the student, clarification and strengthening of convictions and beliefs which provide personal identity...It is the factor of believing, of the involvement of the affective as well as cognitive aspects of the self, that distinguishes professional education in theology from other forms of professional education.[11]

The teacher of theology has the responsibility of fulfilling this double goal of educating Christians who will both understand their faith, and live it. This is not a job for just anyone who happens to be academically qualified; it is the vocation of someone who has been called to study the word of God and the tradition of the Church, and who strives every day to integrate that intellectual knowledge with his or her own relationship with God.

Teaching Theology and the Vocation of Teacher

Can teaching theology be considered a vocation? We are all called to holiness, to live a Christian life in the world, and to conform to Christ's image and likeness.[12] Each of us fulfills the call to holiness in a different way. As the Second Vatican Council teaches, "the forms and tasks of life are many, but holiness is one."[13] One of the forms that a vocation may take is that of a teacher of theology: to live the word of God and the truths of the faith, and to teach the word and the truths. In the theologian's vocation, the two aspects exist by which one recognizes a vocation: to live God's call in our everyday lives, and to spread the Good News. For a teacher of theology, this means to live God's call personally and to teach the word of God in class and through his or her actions.

In the past fifteen years a few documents, both papal and curial, have highlighted the importance of the theology teacher's vocation. These documents repeatedly emphasize the connection between the teacher's professional and spiritual life. There can be no dichotomy or separation between the two. In his apostolic constitution, *Sapientia christiana*, of April 15, 1979, on the norms for ecclesiastical universities and faculties, Pope John Paul II notes:

> Teachers are invested with the very weighty responsibility in fulfilling a special ministry of the word of God and in being instruments of the faith for the young. Let them, above all, therefore be for their students, and for the rest of the faithful, witnesses of the living truth of the Gospel and examples of fidelity to the Church.[14]

After recognizing the importance of the work of teachers, the Pope notes that the most important facet of their teaching is to be "witnesses to the living truth of the Gospel." How are they going to accomplish that goal without a vibrant personal faith and a strong sense of vocation in who they are and what they do? The constitution ends with norms regulating the hiring of teachers. Teachers of theology must "be distinguished by wealth of knowledge, witness of life, and a sense of responsibility." In addition, they must demonstrate teaching and research abilities.[15] Thus, there is a balance to be achieved between a teacher's academic credentials, and the essential fact of having a strong, personal, active faith. All these aspects are the professional prerequisites for a teacher of theology. And only the teacher who can achieve the balance between academic knowledge and lived faith will be truly effective.

On August 15, 1990 Pope John Paul II published the apostolic constitution *Ex corde Ecclesiae* on Catholic universities. In this text, he stresses that

> [u]niversity teachers should seek to improve their competence and endeavor to set the content, objectives, methods and results of research in an individual discipline within the framework of a coherent world vision. Christians among teachers are called to be witnesses and educators of authentic Christan life, which evidences an attained integration between faith and life, and between professional competence and Christian wisdom. All teachers are to be inspired by academic ideals and by the principles of an authentically human life.[16]

The important aspect of a Catholic education is the influence of the Christian witness of life of the teachers. The burden that this places on the teachers is that they must be living an authentic and vibrant faith, continually responding to the call of God in their lives. If not, the goal of such an education, to instruct academically and by means of the witness of life, cannot be reached.

On May 24, 1990 the Congregation for the Doctrine of the Faith issued an instruction on the ecclesial vocation of the theologian. In this document, the Congregation highlights the point that to teach theology is to teach both the reasons of the faith and faith itself.[17] Perhaps most importantly, the document states, "the commitment to theology requires a spiritual effort to grow in virtue and holiness."[18] This growth in holiness, to which we are all called, is especially important for the teacher of theology who strives to understand his or her own relationship with God in light of the truths that he or she teaches, and who must impart a living faith to his or her students. Being a Christian and living a Christian life does not necessarily equip one to teach theology; nor does the fact that a person knows all the theoretical, academic aspects of theology: the balance between the two must always be achieved.

Academic Teaching and Formation

What, then, does it mean to be a teacher of theology? Above all else, it involves teaching the faith and living it as an example. Only through the teacher's own belief and desire for holiness will the faith be adequately transmitted. The truth of this statement applies not only to the basic concepts of the faith taught in catechesis, but also to the more complex realities that are studied in the theological disciplines. If a teacher does not experience the living Church through a strong faith, what can he or she teach to the students of this reality?

Every teacher must know his or her academic material well. One cannot expect to be able to impart knowledge without a solid professional background. At the same time, it is equally important for the teacher of theology to be a living witness to this faith that he or she is teaching. Teaching is more than an intellectual exercise; everything a person believes and lives comes out in his or her teaching. Much of the message that is taught does not come from the subject matter itself, but through the person of the teacher. What is his or her lifestyle? How does he or she live his or her faith? How does he or she treat the students and other teachers?

The Vocation of the Teacher of Theology

What is the meaning and purpose of the theology teacher's vocation? "Teachers teach to make a difference in the lives of their students. They want their students to learn something."[19] What is the difference that the teacher of theology makes in the life of his or her students? What is it that these students will learn? What is their deepest need? All students of theology need to reflect on their faith, on their vocations as Christians, on the practice of their faith, as well as on the role of their faith and its practice in the community.[20]

In order to achieve these goals, teachers of theology must integrate their vocation to teach with their academic qualifications and life of faith. Their first priority is to follow Christ's call to discipleship. As Christians, they seek to fulfill the will of God in their lives and to bear witness to Christ in all that they do. As teachers of theology, they preach the word of God and work toward the sanctification of both themselves and their students.[21] Teachers of theology are educators: they teach students both the intellectual aspects of theology and the lived experience of the faith.

Many studies have been written on educational methods dealing with such questions as what is the purpose of teaching theology and how can theology be most effectively taught. One author notes that although curriculum, course content, teaching techniques, etc. are all important in the process of learning, the most important factor in teaching theology effectively is

> that [the subject matter] had in some instance personal significance to the instructor, that it was critical to the life and mission of the Church, that it pertained ultimately to critical issues in the lives of people, that historical matters could shed light on contemporary issues, and the like... theological education is effective when theology is for the theological educator a cognitive disposition and orientation of the soul, a wisdom which can be promoted, deepened, and extended by human study and argumentation....

The focus is still on the subject matter more than on the teacher or the student, but the subject matter is communicated in such a way that more than information is transmitted, that more than acute logical arrangement is displayed, that more than immediate applicability to specific pastoral problems is offered.[22]

In the same vein, a study done in 1956 noted that being a teacher of theology involves more than teaching an academic discipline. There is also an element of formation: the professor is a model and he or she forms the students.[23] But the professor is not only a model or an example to be emulated; he or she must also teach the students:

Good teaching...brings the student to see a particular subject in the context of the Christian faith so that he discovers his personal commitment to be bound up with what he is 'studying.' The objectivity which is required is not lost. Rather, the objective search of teacher and student is carried one step further so that together they face the ultimate issues of the Church's faith as approached through the particular subject in hand. The message of the prophets becomes alive for contemporary issues when the student learns to interpret the prophets in their time and discovers the relationship between the Word of God as it came to them and the issues of the common life today.[24]

Teaching, especially in matters of faith, is a two-way street: teachers both communicate the faith and receive challenges for growth in their own faith. It takes courage to be a good teacher, to open oneself up to learning from one's students and colleagues.

T. H. Groome adds a helpful insight when he points out that the teacher of theology must be more than merely professionally and academically competent.[25] He tells the story of how he was asked by a student studying to be a teacher of religion what is at the heart of good teaching. He wanted to speak of the importance of biblical and theological formation, theory, history, practice, even practical pastoral experience. All these academic and practical elements were important for a theological discipline to be well-taught; but for it to be effectively taught, more was needed; the subject needed the "heart" of a teacher. The teacher's own spiritual and religious life were recognized as essential to the successful teaching of theology.[26]

Groome develops this metaphor of the heart by pointing out four essential elements of the religious educator: passion, generosity, love, and commitment. A teacher of theology needs *passion* for the students, reverence for them as human beings, as "co-learners" on spiritual journeys. The *generosity* of the teacher of theology is his or her hospitality in creating a learning environment in which the students can learn. The teacher of theology must have a *love* for the tradition of the Church. The teacher's love for and knowledge of the tradition of the Church is part of his or her mandate to remember and hand on the faith; this same love of tradition helps the teacher to hand on the faith to his or her students. The students can only grow in love of their faith if they know and understand it.[27] Finally, the teacher of theology must have a *commitment* to the reign of God: the reign of God is a "statement of our purpose." This is what we are about, why we educate. With this goal in mind, our teaching must necessarily be practical: teaching not only academic concepts, but a way of life.[28] These four characteristics "will profoundly shape how we educate and what we educate for. The level to which they are reflected in our educational praxis will be both the measure and the source of our own holiness."[29] In these four goals is the balance to be attained between an academic and intellectual mastery of one's subject and the lived experience of faith.

The search for holiness to which we are all called is the source of the vocation of the teacher of theology. Why else teach such a discipline except to enrich one's relationship with God and to grow in life with God, in holiness? If this is so, then the teacher's relationship with God must shine through everything he or she teaches.

> We are more prone…to speak glibly about [spirituality] for others and less likely to reflect on the kind of holiness asked

of us by the very form of service that we render as religious educators. Yet our attempts to be spiritual guides must surely be grounded in our own spiritual journeys. It is not possible to lead people out (e-ducare) religiously if we are not traveling in that direction ourselves.[30]

The teacher of theology has the obligation to grow in holiness, through his or her relationship with God as well as through his or her encounters with the students, the "co-learners."

Living as a Christian in the World

In teaching theology, the teacher challenges people to be mature Christians. For this very reason, he or she should not be afraid of approaching the modern world in which the students live, the society in which they are living out their Christian beliefs. It used to be thought that the best way of teaching Christians was to keep them away from the world, lest they be contaminated by it. This cannot be; it can all too easily fall apart. Everyone's beliefs must be integrated into their lives and must be continually challenged so that they can respond to the challenges.

The ultimate goal of the teacher of theology is to pass on a twofold help for the Christian living in the modern world: an intellectual knowledge of the history and important events of Christianity, as well as the intellectual tools with which to make spiritual and moral decisions and to live a mature faith life. This can be done by relating the intellectual and academic knowledge to the personal situations of the students, and also to the situation of the Christian community in the world. The personal lives of the students, as well as the life of the world around us, need to be reflected on in light of our tradition and our beliefs, so that all aspects of life will be integrated.[31]

The important goal is to make the student bring his or her mature faith into a conversation with the world. Christians should interact with the world around them, to grow from and be challenged by it, and to challenge the world to grow.

The theological teacher must continually be pushing students to examine the ultimate presuppositions with which they think and with which they judge themselves and their fellows. No purely technical mastery of logic or method will suffice. In theology we are dealing with issues which involve conviction and faith. A teacher of history who brings historical periods vividly to life, and who contributes important knowledge of historical movements, has not led students to the depth of his subject until the question of the meaning of this history has been raised. How are historical causes and events to be understood and what is the relation of a Christian view of human events to other views? Such questions ought to be inescapable in a theological course.[32]

The teacher of theology must try to integrate the life of the Church with the lives that people live in the world. People have to address so many difficulties, problems, joys, and confusions in their lives; learning theology should help them to integrate their faith with their everyday living. There can be no isolation from the world and society.[33] Learning theology should equip the student to approach the world, learn from it, and bring his or her experience and understanding of God to it.

Keeping the Vocation Alive

How does a teacher of theology ensure that he or she is continually growing and trying to follow his or her vocation? Among the many different approaches one could take, I would like to extrapolate on some interesting ideas provided by Esther de Waal. In her book, *Seeking God: The Way of St. Benedict*, she examines the Benedictine Rule and applies the concepts to daily life. She considers the ideas of listening to God's voice in our lives, being bound by stability so that we cannot run away from a difficult situation but we must face it and grow from the challenges God is offering us, being able to adapt to changes that arise, and being able to find a balance. Many of these ideas could be particularly addressed to the life of the teacher of theology.

The teacher must be grounded in stability, in his or her life with God. This stability allows one the freedom to embrace the world and its questions and difficulties; it allows one the freedom to be challenged. The challenge is to never become complacent or stale, either in one's approach to the material being taught, or in one's spiritual life. Daily routines can become humdrum, especially if we are not open to seeing our vocation challenged and deepened in daily, even repetitious events.

In a similar vein, another author discusses the concept of enclosure. Dom Sighard Kleiner speaks of the value of being apart, in a place of one's own that is inaccessible to the public. In order to be creative, and perhaps even effective, everyone needs a place of independence, a place to gather his or her resources. Everyone needs to retreat in order "to meet the Lord," to discover himself or herself as a child of God, and to learn how to better love and serve others.[34] In the writings of St. Benedict,[35] the enclosure spoken of is the physical one of the monastery. However, it must be understood as more than merely physical enclosure. In everyone's life there must be at least a spiritual enclosure, a place to which one can retreat to be with God and deepen that relationship and source of strength.[36] This place or relationship must be carefully guarded and its importance for the vocation of the teacher must be recognized. Without caring daily for the source of one's vocation, one's motivation can all too easily fade or wither away.

We must also be careful of attributing too much importance to our work. Teachers of theology perform an important task. Their work, however, must be seen in relation to their lives and to their place in the community of believers, the people of God. If we value our teaching and our insights without always remembering why we are teaching and in what context we live, our work will become an end in itself. Once again, Esther de Waal makes some insightful comments:

> ...work...is to be kept in proportion by prayer and by study. There is no chance here for work to develop, or to degenerate, into activism...By breaking off to pray St. Benedict is making sure that work does not become an end in itself, an idol dominating everything else. And he is

equally on his guard against another danger closely akin to that, work being entirely with reference to the self, a process of self-fulfillment. Work is always seen in its communal context. The point at which the craftsman 'becomes puffed up by his skillfulness in his craft and feeling that he is conferring something on the monastery' is the point at which he is to be removed from practicing it. The expert is so to exercise his skill that he benefits the whole; he must work in the spirit of respect both for his material and for his fellow men. The satisfaction lies in the work itself and not in the personal recognition that it brings to its creator.[37]

Again we return to the central issue: the balance that is required in the life of a teacher of theology between academic excellence and the growing life of faith. One cannot outshine the other, or develop separately from the other. They must be held in tension so that they can complement and feed each other.

Conclusion

Think back to your favorite course or teacher in high school or college. What was it that made that course come alive for you? What is it that makes you remember that teacher? What affected you about that teacher? Often it is the passion the teacher had for the subject. Even if the subject seemed dull or tedious at first, it became interesting and alive because of the teacher's enthusiasm. The same is doubly true for the teacher of theology: a passion for the subject is required to make it come alive for the students. Where can that passion be found? In the call from God to teach and use this knowledge, to make the knowledge of God and of the Church not just an intellectual undertaking, but a lived, personal, and vibrant knowledge.

Teachers of theology must question whether their intellectual and faith lives feed one another to form a whole. Or whether they are living their lives in two spheres, the professional and the spiritual, which never connect. Professional, academic lives must be grounded in spiritual lives of faith if they are to be truly responding to the call of being a teacher. Our spiritual lives and sense of vocation must flow through every part of our lives. As a teacher of spirituality or moral theology, I am following God's call: he has called me to this task and, thus, it must be more than a mere intellectual exercise, more than a job. Because I have been called to be a teacher, I must always be aware of and responding to this call. Like all Christians, I must live the gospel as fully as I can and that must radiate in everything I do.

As a teacher, I am called to teach the academic content of the course, as well as to be a witness to Christ in the way that I live and how I approach my teaching, my students, and my colleagues. If I separate my teaching from my sense of who God is calling me to be, or if I allow my teaching to become a dry intellectual exercise and not an expression of my life of faith, I will not teach my discipline effectively. Like all memorable teachers, I must have passion for my subject. In the case of a theology teacher, passion for one's subject entails a passion for God and for a life lived in God.

Being professionals does not mean that we must separate ourselves from our vocations. On the contrary, profession and vocation are not opposed; they should complement one another. Every teacher must demonstrate professional competence; every Christian must live out the vocation to which he or she has been called. That vocation must be nourished by a living faith which is the root and center of his or her life. A vocation is a call that both transforms and obligates a person. It is not sufficient simply to teach. The material presented in class must be accurate and well-presented academically; in addition, it must radiate an active faith life.

A sense of one's vocation is necessary to all aspects of a person's life. With particular reference to the vocation of a teacher of theology, one author cautions about

…the fundamental dialectic between the witness of scripture and classical Christian tradition, on the one side, and the fabric of our daily lives, on the other. Rediscovering this dialectic lies, therefore, at the center of what it means to be called a professor of theology…[38]

It is precisely in this challenge that the life of a teacher of theology must be centered: to never lose one's love of God and of the Church, to teach the truths of tradition, and to radiate the fact that those truths are alive in our lives, in our close relationship to God.

SUGGESTED READING

Fleischer, B. J. "The Ignatian Vision for Higher Education: Practical Theology," *Religious Education* 88(1993): 255–73.

Groome, T. H. "The Spirituality of the Religious Educator." *Religious Education* 83(1988): 9–20.

Gustafson, J. M. "The Vocation of the Theological Educator." *Theological Education, Supplement* (1987): 53–68.

Hall, D.J. "Theological Education as Character Formation." *Theological Education, Supplement* 1(1988): 53–79.

Hough, Jr., J.C. and J. B. Cobb, Jr. *Christian Identity and Theological Education*. Chico, Calif.: Scholars Press, 1985.

Kleiner, Dom S. *Serving God First. Insights on the Rule of St. Benedict*. Translated by James Scharinger. Cistercian Series, no. 83. Kalamazoo, Mich.: Cistercian Publications, 1985.

Lindbeck, G. "Spiritual Formation and Theological Formation." *Theological Education, Supplement* 1(1988): 10–32.

McDonagh, E. *The Making of Disciples. Tasks of Moral Theology*. Wilmington, Del.: Michael Glazier, 1982.

Niebuhr, H. R., D. D. Williams, and J. M. Gustafson. *The Advancement of Theological Education*. New York: Harper, 1957.

Trainor, M. "Images of the Faith Educator." *Religious Education* 86(1991): 285–91.

Waal, Esther de. Seeking God: *The Way of St. Benedict*. Collegeville, Minn.: The Liturgical Press, 1984.

Walters, T. P. "Instructional Objectives, Cathechesis and the Future." *Religious Education* 85(1990): 84–91.

Wood, C. M. "'Spiritual Formation' and 'Theological Education.'" *Religious Education* 86(1991): 550–61.

Chapter Four

Listening to God Within

CHRISTOPHER O'DONNELL, O.CARM.

Of the many crises facing the Church at this time, three are more important for our theme. The world, often called "post-Christian," is harshly secular and would seem to leave little room for the message of the Gospel as it affects either belief or morals. Allied with secularism, there is in the first world a pervasive liberal ethic which gives individual freedom of choice such a supreme value that moral norms are resented and rejected if they appear to infringe the individual's right to be self-fulfilled. A third danger, at an opposite pole to these two, is the new religiosity, which in its myriad forms is attracting millions. Even when it is not hostile to Christianity, the new religiosity, especially in New Age manifestations, often presents a world vision which is ultimately incompatible with the core values of the Gospel.

Alongside these three crises, there is the evident one of people becoming disaffected with the Church and its teachings. More serious, because more common and ultimately more radical, is the apathy which has overtaken many Catholics. It is not, however, so much that they do not believe, as they do not see the point of believing. The crisis here is not particularly one of faith, but one of religious experience; having no personal contact with the living God, millions are drifting away. At a distance of some decades one can appreciate the acuity of vision in one of the most quoted of all the statements of Karl Rahner, "The devout

Christian of the future will either be a 'mystic,' one who has 'experienced' something, or he will cease to be anything at all."[1]

Moral Theology and Prayer

It would seem then that a reflection on morality and prayer would have an important contribution to make to the Church of today. If we look, however, at what the classical manuals of moral theology actually have to say about prayer, we will rarely find anything that inspires or in any way enkindles devotion. For the most part, these once relevant but now dusty pastoral tomes merely outline the duty, kinds, conditions, and necessity of prayer.[2] Little, if anything, is ever said about the intrinsic connection between an authentic life of prayer and growth in the moral life. This is the way it was for centuries. A noticeable change to this sad state of affairs did not come until just before the Second Vatican Council, when authors like Bernard Häring stressed the priority of love over law in the ongoing renewal of moral theology. In his writings and in those of other contemporary moral theologians, prayer was treated far more extensively and at greater depth than in the manuals and other derivative works.[3] To back up their claims, they found that the classical authors like St. Alphonsus Liguori—himself often referred to as "The Doctor of Prayer"—had a much more profound teaching on prayer than the manualists who followed them.[4]

That is not to say that a completely different way of viewing the relationship between morality and prayer took effect overnight. To be sure, many authors still saw prayer as an expression of Christian morality, rather than one of its very foundations. Even today there are presentations of morality, even authoritative ones, which still stress the moral law as the means for achieving full human development in Christ, without, however, sufficiently indicating the essential place of prayer in this spiritual process. Be that as it may, the view gradually held sway that prayer was essential for us to appropriate our human authenticity and be in a position to act out a fundamental Christian choice for life in and from the Divine Mystery.[5] Indeed, we have begun in the past three decades to find writings which have developed the role of prayer and its consequences for the whole of Christian life.[6] In this literature, prayer is no longer merely a matter of one's personal relationship with God, but also involves social, and in places even political, commitment in the service of the Kingdom and in love of our brothers and sisters.[7]

Founded on Prayer

If we see prayer not as a moral task, but as a foundation of the whole moral life, a superficial notion of prayer will not suffice. A few hurried moments of intercessory or petitionary prayer will not ground the Christian's search for authenticity of life. There are many definitions of prayer. The classical one from John Damascene united three descriptions that had become established even in his time: "Prayer is an ascent of the mind to God, or the asking God for things which are fitting."[8] But this definition needs to be teased out. It could be understood in a shallow way as indicating what we do, rather than what the Holy Spirit does in us. A definition of St. Gregory of Sinai (d. 1360) brings us closer to the profound reality: "Prayer is the manifestation of baptism."[9] Baptism inserts us into the life of the Trinity. We are baptized *into* (in Greek: *eis*) the person (or name) of the Father and of the Son and of the Holy Spirit (Mt 28:19). There are henceforth a new set of relations with each of the divine persons: we are children of the Father; we are brothers and sisters of Jesus the Son; we are temples of the Holy Spirit.

Christian prayer is not a matter of our own initiative, but a response to the love of God poured out into our hearts through the Holy Spirit who has been given to us (cf. Rom 5:5). Baptism is a re-creation in the image and likeness of God (cf. Gen 1:27); in Christ we are a new creation (cf. 2 Cor 5:17). Both morality and prayer express this fundamental reality. For Paul, morality is not so much a matter of obeying the law, even God's law, as of acting out what we have become through baptism: "...you must consider yourselves dead to sin but alive for God in Christ Jesus" (Rom 6:11); "...you are not in the flesh, you are in the Spirit since the Spirit of God dwells in you" (Rom 8:9). Our deepest prayer is that of the Spirit who prays within us (cf. Rom 8:26). Reflecting on his own experience and on the New Testament, St. Augustine himself spoke of prayer as desire for God: "for your desire itself is your prayer, and if your desire is continuous, so is your prayer."[10] There is always the danger that we try to use prayer as a way of manipulating God for our purposes; the desire for God allows prayer to form us according to God's plan for us.

If we look to the tradition of the Christian East, we see yet another way of considering prayer. Central to the Eastern view of humanity is the doctrine of divinization (*theôsis*), the grounds for which are clearly found in the New Testament.[11] We have been set free from the corruption of that which is in the world in order to become "sharers in the divine nature" (2 Pet 1:4). The Christian life is conceived of as a progressive divinization, so that the image of God is perfected in us until we reach final glory. This divinization is anticipated in, and brought about through, the Eucharist. Its classical exposition is in St. Athanasius (d. 373): "God became man, so that we might become God."[12]

Growth in Prayer

Prayer, like life, never stands still: it either grows or diminishes.[13] Since we relate to God largely through prayer, how we pray is often a good indication of the depth of our relationship with God. Most of us usually begin to pray out of a sense of obligation. As children we are told that it is a good thing to pray, that it is our duty, and that we should not neglect it. We are taught to place our needs and the needs of others before God. We are taught set prayers such as the Our Father, the Hail Mary, and the Glory Be to the Father. We memorize such prayers and recite them faithfully morning, noon, and night, day-in and day-out.

At this stage, prayer is a moment in the day, something we do for the purpose of getting what we want or (perhaps less selfishly) of doing something pleasing to God. At times, we realize that it is appropriate to ask pardon of God for our sins.

The image of God underlying such prayer is that of a beneficent God who cares for us and about us. When we sin, however, a negative image of God can creep in. God can seem like a policeman or a wrathful judge, who watches out for our faults and punishes us for them by exacting every last measure of recompense. Some people seem never to get beyond this stage. Although it represents only a rudimentary level of the spiritual life, even this stage expresses a number of profound values. It reflects, for example, the most basic of all religious truths, namely that God is transcendent and that we are needy creatures. It can also hold the important truth that God saves by forgiving us and that with God all things are possible (cf. Mt 19:26). There are, nevertheless, still some weaknesses associated with remaining at this stage. Prayer can be compartmentalized, being just one of the things we do. It can lack sincerity and, if we are not careful, even involve us in subtle forms of self-deception. It can distort our image of God, making it at times nothing more than an exaggerated caricature or a stale stereotype. Such prayer can be thought of as nothing more than a duty, something that can be neglected or, worse yet, even ignored. More importantly, this type of prayer does not answer our deepest need; it fails to fill us with a passion for God that would take hold of us and dominate our lives.[14]

A Change of Heart

Movement from this early way of prayer is often associated with some critical moment in one's life. It may be some deep awareness of God's love, a newly discovered sense of inadequacy, an experience of awe about God. Very often it can be a time of turmoil or suffering that shakes our faith and in the process deepens it. For some people, it can be the occasion of a retreat, an encounter with the Charismatic Renewal with the experience of "Baptism in the Holy Spirit"; for some of the saints, it was a sermon they heard or a book they read.

Characteristic of such turning points is a paradoxical recasting of our beliefs. God becomes much greater than we had ever

imagined and closer to us than we had ever experienced. These
critical turning points may be called by the more traditional term
"conversion moments." But conversion is ultimately not our
initiative, but our response to grace. And this response of the heart
finds expression not only in life, but in prayer. It is here perhaps
that we have the most significant basis of morality. Our lives are to
reflect more and more the life of God. Moral precepts are no
longer external to us, but are exigencies that arise from our very
being which is being transformed in order to share in the divine
nature. Those who prayerfully contemplate this overwhelming
truth will come to that conversion which is described by Bernard
Lonergan as "being-in-love with God,"[15] which is ultimately
nothing else than a full acceptance of the meaning of our baptism.
Thus, St. John of the Cross writes:

> He conferred the power of becoming children of God (only)
> to those born of God, who in their rebirth through grace and
> death to everything of the old man, rise above themselves
> to the supernatural and receive from God this rebirth and
> sonship which transcends everything imaginable…To be
> reborn of the Holy Spirit during this life is to become most
> like God in purity.[16]

Generally speaking, Christian spirituality places much
emphasis on conversion of the heart.[17] The heart is the battle-
ground of good and evil; it is in the heart that God dwells. The
theologies of East and West stress the significance of the heart in
the moral life in different ways. Whereas, in the West, we tend to
focus on the heart's detachment from individual sins—both
mortal and venial—in the East, believers are much more concerned with the individual's habitual disposition.[18] For them,
virtue is not so much a series of good acts, but a state (*katastasis*)
that orients the heart toward God. Various traditions employ
different means to show how our hearts are directed to God and
open to his loving invasion. The Benedictine tradition, for example, relies on the Word of God to clear the heart for God. The
Ignatian tradition, in turn, places great emphasis on the discernment of the workings in the heart of the various spirits. The

Eastern tradition constantly speaks of attention to the heart. The Carmelite tradition by and large stresses that one surrenders the heart to God and then one gets on with living in faith, hope, and love.

Trinitarian Prayer

Ultimately, our hearts will find rest only in the God who is Father, Son, and Spirit. Trinitarian prayer should be cultivated by everyone. One can, of course, say that all authentic prayer is Trinitarian: it is in the Spirit, through the Son, and reaching toward the the Father. But very often the Trinitarian dimension is only implicit. When it becomes explicit, there ensues great enchantment. From merely affirming an intellectual formula—three Persons in one God—we open out and develop deeply enriching relationships with each of the Persons. Such was the prayer of St. Catherine of Siena (d. 1380), who saw the Father as power and goodness, the Son as wisdom, and the Spirit as mercy.[19]

Trinitarian prayer is not a retreat into silence like Buddhist prayer. Nor is it a simple acknowledgment of God's greatness, his goodness, and his right to be served as in Islam. It is even more than the great Hebrew prayer and profession of faith, the Sh'ema: "Hear, O Israel! The Lord is our God, the Lord alone! Therefore, you shall love the Lord, your God, with all your heart, and with all your soul, and with all your strength" (Dt 6:4–9).[20] It seeks, first and foremost, to know the Father's "fountain-like love" (amor fontalis).[21] It is a prayer of trust, accepting the Creator as one deeply concerned with us, with an eternal plan in which we are the recipients of mercy and love. The Christian comes to know Jesus as Lord and Savior, the one who died for us and is not ashamed to call us his brothers and sisters (cf. Heb 2:11). Gradually, the Christian becomes aware of being a temple of the Spirit, and of the Spirit being "Helper and Guide,"[22] or in the language of St. Thomas Aquinas, our "Friend."[23]

A Pearl Beyond Price—But for All?

It is the unanimous teaching of the mystics that the way to union or friendship with God is truly a pearl beyond all price that incomparably satisfies the desires of the human heart. The inner journey to seek the triune God within the depths of our hearts is the supreme beatitude possible on this earth. Their teaching, however, is extremely realistic: to find God we have to be prepared to abandon all that is contrary to his will; to be united to God we need to be purified; to know the joy of the Lord, we have to turn from the false joys offered by sin and selfishness.

But has this teaching of the mystics a relevance for the "ordinary" Christian? The majority of Catholics may not have the courage to abandon sin and selfishness in a way that would dispose them to receive the supremely satisfying gifts that God offers to those who respond profoundly to divine love. The mystics, however, are not just specially gifted people whom God has specially chosen to give his choicest favors. They are also paradigmatic for the Church. Theirs is the way of following Christ. For many centuries the Church has been infiltrated by a serious practical error that there are two calls within Christ's body: one to an ordinary Christian life; the other, to profound holiness. To remedy this misleading impression, the fathers of the Second Vatican Council formulated in chapter five of "The Dogmatic Constitution on the Church" the well-known magisterial teaching now commonly referred to as "the universal call to holiness."[24]

Beyond this universal call, the Church must further teach in the area of spirituality what theologians of liberation have discovered in their field: people are enriched as soon as they undertake the struggle (*lucha*) for liberation. Similarly, those who become conscious of the wonder of their baptism and begin to pray according to its implications are already greatly blessed. The inner journey has its trials, but once it is seriously undertaken, one already starts to experience its rewards. We may be far from the highest mystical graces and find ourselves plodding along in distracted darkness, but even this preliminary stage begins to give meaning to our lives and to draw us out of ourselves to God who is both utterly transcendent and profoundly immanent. It is here, when we least expect it, that contemplative prayer breaks into our lives.

Contemplation is a word with many meanings; it is one of the longest entries in the standard work of reference, *Dictionnaire de spiritualité*.[25] At its heart is the sense of gazing on God and allowing him to look on us.[26] Many people achieve contemplative prayer through developed vocal prayer, such as the Rosary. There are indeed a multitude of ways, but what unites them all is a journey toward God, a reaching toward him in response to his love and loveliness. It implies some surrender, always to be perfected, to his will. Contemplation is the essential fundamental form of Christian prayer.[27] It is also an indispensable component of liturgical worship, as the well-known book of H. U. von Balthasar asserts—the German title of which is not *Prayer*, but *Contemplative Prayer*.[28] One of the critical weaknesses of the post-Vatican II Church has been its failure to set contemplative prayer before believers as a great adventure and something that is ultimately satisfying. An emphasis on participation in the liturgy is itself insufficient unless people are taught to look upon God and on themselves in the light of his glory. The journey inward to where God dwells in our heart is an essential predisposition for the journey outward in liturgy and missionary love.

Prayer and the Moral Life

Two bold texts, one from the East and one from the West, indicate the tight nexus between prayer and the moral life. Theophane the Recluse (d. 1894) writes:

Prayer is the test of everything; prayer is also the source of everything; prayer is the driving force of everything; prayer is also the director of everything. If prayer is right, everything is right. For prayer will not allow anything to go wrong.[29]

This text may seem to contradict experience. We all know that people can engage in a lot of prayer and yet have their lives in moral disorder. But what Bishop Theophane suggests is surely that eventually prayer will gradually bring a person around to God's will. It is impossible to face God daily in silent prayer and remain obstinately in opposition to his love. It may take time, but prayer has the power to transform moral attitudes and finally produce a conversion. A common occurrence, however, is that someone with a serious problem will abandon prayer rather than endure the pain of daily facing God with his or her own sinful self.

For a Western text we can take a passage from the book she wrote for her sisters, *The Way of Perfection*, where St. Teresa of Avila is at pains to stress the importance of mental prayer (chaps. 21–23), stating clearly: "Don't let anybody deceive you by showing you a road other than that of prayer."[30] There is no spiritual growth unless we come to know God, to surrender our hearts to Trinitarian love, and to come to know ourselves; such self-knowledge and submission are probably impossible for most people without serious prayer. If we seek to know ourselves merely by psychological analysis, by simple introspection, by analyzing our motivation in various circumstances, then the inner self we discover will scarcely be an integral one. Either we shall be crushed by the negativity we find in ourselves, or we may bypass what is unlovely in our thoughts, acts, and feelings.

A whole view of the human person is one in which good and evil are both recognized as present. We need, however, to know how to change, how to be healed, how to come into authenticity. Human authenticity is not the same as psychological wholeness; people may be quite damaged from a psychological point of view, and yet have a human integrity, a meaning in their lives, profound contentment, even in the pain of psychological inadequacy. The difference here is prayer. When we merely look within, we find ourselves, and the discovery may be disturbing. If we look inside ourselves, and find ourselves as temples of the Trinity, then we have a basic optimism about our being. We discover the power of the confirmation gift of reverence ("piety and fear of the Lord"). This leads to new possibilities of relating to ourselves and others, who in their turn are also temples of the Spirit.

This Trinitarian discovery allows us to view reality from the side of God.[31] Morality is no longer something external, but arises from a participation in God's vision of ourselves and of the world. The motivation for moral behavior will thence be the quiet voice of God within us drawing us to goodness rather than a code of goodness intellectually perceived. This discovery of the Trinity in our lives gives a new foundation to morality. The moral life is no longer a set of precepts, nor even a path to human wholeness, but is a joyful response in love to the God whose love we know in our hearts. Those who are in love find that service of the other is no longer a burden. The deep sense of Trinitarian life within us will lead us to want to be moral. We may at times feel drawn to sin, and indeed fall into its clutches, but the inner drawing power of God will not leave us either to continue in sin, or to despair of freedom from it. The highest pursuit of morality is through contemplative prayer and the laying down of our lives for others.[32]

Conclusion

Many people drop away from the Church and Christ because they have been short-changed by what Bishop Juan Hervas, a founder of the Cursillo Movement, called "the minimalist corruption of Christianity." A Christianity presented as the observance of the commandments and Sunday Mass could be called degenerate: it fails to present the possibility of true beatitude even in this life; it gives little inkling of the joy that is to be had from following the way of Christ; it does not succeed in bringing us into the wonder of our being inhabited by the Triune God or into "the surpassing knowledge of my Lord Christ Jesus" (Phil 3:8).

People today need to know how to ascend to God in the classical definition of prayer. There is a growing disillusionment with reason, with science, and with wealth as ways in which humans can achieve happiness or ultimate meaning. There are significant studies showing that those who pray are significantly happier than those who do not.[33] More and more are turning to New Age spiritualities to seek a transformation of their lives.[34]

Though many of its values may be seen as ambiguous, the whole New Age package is ultimately neo-Gnostic and Pelagian. Its morality does not go beyond a liberal ethic. As John Drane notes, "It (the New Age) also has apparently the power to address the needs of women and men in today's world in a way that the Church has long since lost."[35]

Yet in the Catholic tradition we have untold riches that will satisfy the human heart in ways far surpassing what the New Age has to offer. The Church needs to open people's eyes to the intimate sharing in the life of the Trinity that their baptismal dignity affords them. It needs to teach prayer even more urgently than to instill morality.[36] An older generation can often be heard complaining about modern catechetics that children do not know the commandments. One is tempted to reply, "But do they really know Christ Jesus?" for if they truly do, the commandments will in time appear to them as a way of love that they will cheerfully embrace.

SUGGESTED READING

Ancilli, E. ed. *La preghiera. Bibbia, teologia, esperienze storiche.* 2nd ed. 2 vols. Rome: Città Nuova, 1990.

Balthasar, H. U. von. *Prayer.* San Francisco: Ignatius Press, 1986.

Bastianel, S. *Prayer in Christian Moral Life.* Slough: St. Paul, 1988.

Blommestijn, H. "Discovering the Self and the World through the Eyes of God. A Selective Reading of 'The Spiritual Canticle.' " *Studies in Spirituality* 3(1993): 173–99.

Cameli, L. J. "Preaching and the Teaching of Prayer in Parishes." *Chicago Studies* 31(1992): 3–12.

Compagoni, F., G. Piana and S. Printero, eds. *Nuovo dizionario di teologia morale.* Milan: San Paolo, 1990. S. v. "Preghiera," by G. Piana.

Cunningham, A. "Forms of Prayer in Christian Spirituality." *Chicago Studies* 15(1976): 89–104.

de Marino, A. "Vita morale e spirituale." *Rivista di teologia morale* 24(1992): 231–37.

Drane, J. *What Is the New Age Saying to the Church?* London: Marshall Pickering, 1991.

Giardini, F. "The Growth Process of Christian Prayer Life." *Angelicum* 69(1992): 389–421.

Mongillo, D. "Vita morale e vita mistica." *Rivista di teologia morale* 97(1993): 117–23.

Pikaza, X. *La preghiera cristiana. Sintesi.* Rome: Borla, 1991.

Rahner, K. "Christian Living Formerly and Today." Chap. in *Theological Investigations.* Vol. 17. London/New York: Darton, Longman and Todd / Herder and Herder, 1971.

Studzinski, R. "Prayer and Life." *Chicago Studies* 31(1992): 23–33.

Viller, Marcel, Charles Baumgartner, André Rayez, eds. *Dictionnaire de spiritualité ascétique et mystique, doctrine et histoire.* Paris: Beauchesne, 1937–94. S.v. "Trinité et vie spirituelle," by J. O'Donnell.

Wiseman, J. A. "From Sunday to Weekday: On Praying at All Times." *Chicago Studies* 31(1992): 13–22.

Chapter Five

The Church at Prayer

JAN MICHAEL JONCAS

Earlier essays in this collection have noted the unfortunate consequences for Roman Catholic theology and practice of treating spirituality and morality in disjunction. In the light of Vatican II's assertion that "...all Christians in any state or walk of life are called to the fullness of Christian life and to the perfection of love,"[1] one cannot justify a division of labor in which "spiritual theology" concentrates on a "call to perfection" issued only to an elite in orders and/or religious life, while "moral theology" focuses on the minimum standards of behavior expected of the masses. Both spiritual and moral theologians must attend each other's disciplines as they seek to reflect upon and engender authentic Christian life.

Unfortunately, liturgical practice and study has also developed in problematic relationship with other theological disciplines, reaping similarly unfortunate consequences. Some authors have considered the liturgy as the outward ceremonial and prescribed texts approved for common worship by ecclesiastical authority; liturgics was then studied as a branch of canon law. Other thinkers viewed the study of liturgy as an exercise in antiquarianism and situated it as a segment of Church history. Still others treated the liturgy as a collection of rubrics without theological import and positioned its study among the practical skills needed by clerics. Systematic theologians tended to "raid" the liturgy for individual texts to support their theses, much as they inclined to "prooftext" scripture. When the liturgy was studied as a segment of moral theology, it was often treated as a set of duties embodying the virtue of religion or as a list of conditions for sacramental liceity and validity. It was rarely (if ever) treated in spiritual theology (except as a potentially distressing source of distractions during mental prayer).

Recently, however, a genuine *rapprochement* between liturgical, spiritual, and moral theologians is taking place. As Enda McDonagh notes:

> The renewal of moral theology and its ambition to become a theology of Christian life coincided by and large with the renewed interest in the liturgy and in its theological significance. Since Vatican II this has led to a more self-conscious interest by both moral theologians and liturgists in the interaction between worship and Christian action in the world.[2]

This chapter is an attempt to further that conversation. Firstly, I will sketch some connections between liturgy and Christian life in general. Secondly, I will consider links between liturgy and spirituality: providing a locus for an individual's encounter with the transcendent, union with humanity, and personal spiritual growth. Thirdly, I will consider some connections between liturgy and moral theology: promoting a common vision, critiquing culture, celebrating social transformation.

Liturgy and Christian Life

As is well known, *Sacrosanctum Concilium* [hereafter *SC*] nowhere strictly defines the liturgy. What "The Constitution on the Sacred Liturgy" does present is a series of descriptions, each of which highlights some element of this constitutive component of the Church's life.

The central affirmation about the liturgy appears in *SC*, no. 7. Echoing papal teaching in *Mediator Dei* it states: "the liturgy...is rightly considered as an exercise of Jesus Christ's sacerdotal office."[3] This affirmation puts the emphasis in understanding the liturgy upon mediation. The worship given from and through all eternity to God the Father by Christ Jesus in the Holy Spirit manifests itself in space and time in a twofold but inseparable manner: God manifests Godself to creation and humanity, and humanity and creation respond to God's self-disclosure. The primary mediation of this manifestation and response is in history itself, preeminently in the historical life, deeds, death, and destiny of Jesus of Nazareth. The Church empowered by the Spirit mediates this manifestation and response definitively offered and accepted in Jesus. The liturgy is the interweaving of symbolic texts and ceremonies by which the Church continues to encounter God's self-disclosure and continues to make its loving response to that disclosure. To put it another way, the liturgy has both a "descending" and an "ascending" aspect, articulated as the "sanctification of human beings" and the "glorification of God."[4]

Based on this theological understanding of the liturgy, *SC* sketches the following connections between liturgy and Christian life:

> Sacred liturgy does not exhaust the Church's total activity, for before people can come to liturgy, it is necessary that they be called to faith and to conversion...Thus the Church announces the proclamation of salvation to non-believers, so that all may acknowledge the one true God and Jesus Christ whom he has sent and, doing penance, may be converted from their ways [Jn 17:3; Lk 24:27; Acts 2:38]. To believers as well the Church must preach faith and penance always; moreover the Church must dispose them toward the sacraments, teach them to observe all that Christ has decreed [Mt 28:20], and encourage them to engage in all the works of charity, piety, and the apostolate. By means of these works it will be made manifest that Christ's faithful, though not of this world, are nonetheless to be the light of the world, those who glorify the Father before human beings.
>
> Nonetheless liturgy is the high point toward which the Church's activity tends and it is at the same time the

fountain from which all the Church's power flows. For apostolic labors are ordered toward this: that all made God's children by faith and baptism should come together in unity to praise God in the midst of God's Church, to participate in sacrifice and to eat the Lord's Supper. In turn, this same liturgy impels the faithful that, filled with "the paschal sacraments," they should be "in harmony through piety" [Post-Communion prayer for the Paschal Vigil: *Roman Missal* (hereafter *RM*) 1970/1975]; it prays that "by living they might cling to what they have recognized by faith" [Opening Prayer for Monday within the Octave of Easter: *RM* 1970/1975]. In the Eucharist the renewal of the Lord's covenant with humanity draws the faithful to Christ's unrelenting love and sets them afire [nos. 9–10].[5]

These articles would caution us against three dangers: "pan-liturgism," "empty ritualism," and "anti-liturgism." The Church's life is not exhausted by *leitourgia* (communal worship), but demands *kerygma* (evangelizing proclamation), *didache* (doctrinal reflection), *koinonia* (ecclesial fellowship), and *diakonia* (service to believers, unbelievers and the cosmos). "Being church" cannot be reduced to "attending church." While insisting on the preeminence of the liturgy, *SC* nos. 9–10 recognize the danger of inauthentic worship, demanding that what is celebrated in religious ritual walk apace with what is done by the participants outside of common worship. "Celebrating liturgy" cannot be reduced to "performing rituals." Nevertheless, the Eucharistic liturgy remains the setting in which the Church's life and purpose is most deeply revealed and confirmed, albeit in symbolic and therefore multivalent and mysterious ways. As the old adage puts it: "The Church makes the Eucharist and the Eucharist makes the Church."

Spiritual theologians will note in these articles the emphasis upon transformation under the influence of grace. Since the liturgy is not magic but presupposes the virtue of faith, unbelievers must be called to faith, conversion, change of behavior and attitude as they embark on liturgical worship (cf.

the *Rite of Christian Initiation of Adults*). By means of the liturgy believers are enabled to develop true holiness, "aflame with Christ's insistent love," manifest in their own extra-liturgical acts of piety appropriate to their condition in life.

Moral theologians will note in these texts the corporate character of the Christian life. To be converted from unbelief to belief is a matter not only of an individual's change of behavior and attitude, but also of one's allegiance to a new group, of joining the community of salvation (cf. the *Rite of Christian Initiation of Adults* and the *Rite of Baptism of Infants*). Together, believers are brought beneath God's judgment and are called to relinquish any solidarity with evil (cf. the *Rite of Penance*). Together, believers engage in works of charity and the apostolate (cf. the Lenten disciplines of prayer, fasting, and almsgiving). Together, believers witness to and reaffirm the covenantal foundation of their community's life and behavior every time they celebrate the Eucharist.

Liturgical theologians will note that these themes of individual and corporate transformation in grace focus in the "paschal sacraments." The Church's corporate ritual prayer actualizes not only the power, but also the actual presence-in-mystery of Christ dying, rising, ascending, and pouring forth the Spirit in the gathered assembly. Liturgy as *theologia prima* becomes the bedrock and precondition for *theologia secunda* in whatever form it may take. The doxological foundation and goal of all genuine Christian living and theological reflection demands both participation in and attention to liturgy.

Liturgy and Spiritual Theology

Having considered some general connections between liturgy and Christian life, I would now like to consider in more detail three connections between liturgy and spiritual theology.

1. Encounter with the Transcendent. A theology of revelation notes the multiple ways in which God and humanity encounter each other. From a faith perspective, creation itself presupposes a Creator and is viewed as a locus for God's self-disclosure.

Certain individuals (e.g., Abraham, Moses, the prophets) claim to have encountered God in visions, locutions, dreams, etc.; followers of biblical religion have viewed these encounters as revelatory. The Jewish people came to acknowledge their own corporate history as a prime example of God's revelation. For Christians, the unsurpassable instance of God's revelation occurs in Jesus of Nazareth, whose existence not only points to but embodies the divine-human encounter.

The liturgy celebrates each of these modes of God's self-disclosure. Elements of the material universe (e.g., water, oil, bread, wine, etc.) are taken up into communal prayer as necessary components of liturgical worship. The liturgy does not so much remove these elements from the "profane" sphere of daily life to render them "sacred," as present them before the worshiping community so that all may recognize the prior sacredness of created reality, permeated by the Spirit of God. The Liturgy of the Word recalls, celebrates, and actualizes the individual and communal encounters with God as recorded in the Sacred Scriptures and manifest in the worshiping assembly. But, above all, the liturgy makes present God's greatest self-disclosure in Christ; as *SC*, no. 7 declares:

> He is present in the Sacrifice of the Mass both in the person of the minister...and especially under the eucharistic species. He is present by his power in the sacraments so that when anyone baptizes, Christ himself baptizes [Council of Trent, Session 22: *Doctrine on the Holy Sacrifice of the Mass*, 2]. He is present in his word, for he himself speaks when holy scriptures are read in the church. He is present finally when the Church prays and sings; he himself has promised that "where there are two or three assembled in my name, I am there in the midst of them" [Mt 18:20].[6]

If spiritual theology explores Christian life as the "practice of the presence of God," it should be clear that the liturgy manifests and celebrates that mysterious presence. Through *anamnesis*, the liturgy not only recalls God's great acts in history, but in some way makes them present and powerful for the worshiping assembly. Through *prolepsis*, the liturgy discloses God's absolute future and assures the worshiping assembly that its hope is not in vain by giving them a foretaste of the *eschaton*. Through *epiclesis*, the liturgy transforms the lives of those who gather in the present and equips them to exercise their own proper role in union with Christ in the transformation of the world.

2. *Union with Humanity.* The liturgy also provides a powerful vision of the proper role of human beings in relation to society. On the one hand, unbridled individualism is curbed when all are called to assemble in a common space to recite common texts, sing common chants, assume common postures, make common gestures. On the other hand, the liturgy never submerges individuals in totalitarian exercises of fascist fellow-feeling but cherishes their gifts placed at the service of the common good. The "Poemium" of *General Instruction of the Roman Missal* [hereafter *GIRM*], no. 5 makes this stance abundantly clear:

> The celebration of the Eucharist is an action of the entire Church. In the celebration each person should do all of and only what pertains to him or her, with respect to his or her role within God's people....This people is the people of God, acquired by Christ's blood, assembled by the Lord, nourished by his word, a people called to this: that they might present to God the prayers of the entire human family, a people that gives thanks in Christ for the mystery of salvation by offering his sacrifice, a people that comes together in unity by communion in Christ's body and blood. While by origin it is proper that it should be holy, nonetheless by its conscious, active, and fruitful participation in the mystery of the Eucharist this people continually grows in holiness.[7]

The liturgy images right relation between individuals and society in at least three ways. Firstly, the Christian assembly at its best images a society without economic, racial, or social status division. Access to liturgical worship is premised on faith and baptism, not on one's wealth, skin-color, or prestige. Secondly, the liturgy enshrines human solidarity over time and distance. The texts and ceremonies of the liturgy are the sedimentation of centuries of common prayer linking present worshipers with their ancestors in faith as well as the faith-expression of present believers being linked to those yet to be born. The texts and ceremonies of the liturgy are multi-cultural. The classic Roman Rite boasts influences from Judaism, Hellenism, Late antique Roman society, Frankish civilization, and medieval Christendom and is presently committed to an engagement with contemporary cultures variously termed "adaptation," "indigenization," or "inculturation" (cf. *SC*, nos. 37–40). (In this context, the many non-Roman Western rites and Eastern rites likewise witness to the multi-cultural character of Christian liturgy.) Thirdly, the liturgy teaches worshipers to acknowledge their private concerns in the context of the world's needs, to exercise their common share in the sacerdotal ministry of Christ. For example, both the content and the structure of the General Intercessions promote a non-privatized understanding of Christian prayer:

> In the general intercession or prayer of the faithful the people, exercising their sacerdotal office, pray for all human beings. It is appropriate that this prayer be included in all Masses with the people, so that intercessions might be made for the holy Church, for those in power who govern us, for those beset by various needs, as well as for all human beings and for the salvation of the entire world.

> The order of the intentions as a rule would be:
> a) for the needs of the Church,
> b) for public authorities and the salvation of the world,
> c) for those oppressed by any need,
> d) for the local community...[*GIRM*, nos. 45–46].[8]

3. Personal Spiritual Growth. Finally, the liturgy provides the corporate foundation and context for an individual's spiritual growth. For example, to celebrate the Liturgy of the Hours with regularity and devotion is to be enrolled in the Church's own school of prayer, to embark on a dialogic encounter with the living God:

> The sanctification of human beings is accomplished and worship of God is exercised in the Liturgy of the Hours so that in these activities an exchange or dialogue as it were is established between God and human beings, in which "God is speaking to his people…and his people are responding to God in songs as well as in prayer" [SC, no. 33]. Participants in the liturgy of the hours could be brought to the most abundant holiness through the saving word of God, that receives great stress in it. For the readings are taken from Sacred Scripture, God's words handed on in the psalms are sung in God's sight, and the other intercessions, prayers, and hymns are pervaded by Scripture's spirit and sense. Therefore, not only when those things "that are written for our instruction" [Rom 15:4] are read, but also when the Church prays or sings, the faith of the participants is strengthened [and] their minds are moved toward God, so that they might offer God thoughtful worship and might receive God's grace more abundantly [General Instruction of the Liturgy of the Hours (hereafter GILH), no. 14].[9]

The discipline of praying daily at fixed times not only discloses the sacramental character of time itself, but guarantees that one's engagement with God is not limited to moments of crisis or exultation. Spiritual growth presupposes dedication to the lengthy transformation by which one becomes less self-centered and self-driven and more God-centered and God-empowered. The deliberate decision to make time for God at regular intervals whether or not one "feels" drawn to prayer concretely manifests the choice to make the relationship with God one's highest priority.

Much as the content and structure of the General Intercessions instruct us to place our personal concerns in the context of the world's needs, the structure of the individual hours of the Divine Office tutors us in placing our petitions and intercessions in the context of praise and thanksgiving. Each hour begins with psalmody, enriched at the "hinge" hours of Lauds and Vespers with Old and New Testament Canticles and the Benedictus or Magnificat. Only after blessing and thanking God for God's activity in history do we turn to intercessory and petitionary prayer, confident that what God has accomplished in the past and promised for the future, God will provide. Tendencies toward "works-righteousness" or Pelagianism in the spiritual life are strongly combatted through the wisdom of this prayer-form:

> ...In the liturgy the Church bears the prayers and desires of all the faithful; indeed, it prays for the salvation of the entire world to Christ and, through him, to the Father....And so, not only by charity, modeling and the works of penance, but also by prayer the ecclesial community thus performs the truly maternal office of leading souls to Christ....The Lord alone, without whom we can do nothing, can, having been beseeched by us, give efficacy and increase to our works, so that daily we might be built up into God's temple in the Spirit to the measure of the age of Christ's fullness, and at the same time we might strengthen our determination to bring Christ by means of evangelizing to those outside [*GILH*, nos. 7–18].[10]

Liturgical prayer also provides objectivity and balance in one's spiritual life. Day after day the liturgy invites us to encounter the *mirabilia Dei* in creation, Israel's history, the person of Jesus, the foundational events of the Church through the Scriptures it calls us to chant and ponder. Gradually, the rhythm of our lives mirrors God's cosmic rhythms, purged of sentimentality and egoism. By making the Church's prayer-texts our own, we are steeped in Scripture and molded by its world view. By submitting to the fasts and feasts of the Church's liturgy, we learn a healthy balance of penitential practice and grateful celebration. By observing the liturgical forms, adoration of God, veneration of Mary, honoring of the saints and angels, interceding for the needs of others, and petitioning for oneself reach dynamic spiritual equilibrium.

Liturgy and Moral Theology

The liturgy not only helps to form the spiritual lives of individual believers, it also grounds the corporate life of the Church with significant importance for the moral life of humanity itself.

1. *Promoting a Common Vision.* While the liturgy clearly promotes encounter with God, solidarity with humanity, and individual spiritual growth, it also generates a community of hope-in-action. Social scientists such as Peter Berger have explored how ritual functions in the "social construction of reality" and how religious ritual in particular brings diverse human experiences under a "sacred canopy."[11] Moral theologians in recent years have been exploring the narrative foundations for Christian living, the distinctive vision of reality that undergirds virtuous living and particular decision-making.[12] The liturgy provides Christians with a "plausibility structure" in which the Christian story can become foundational for Christian behavior.

In considering the Christian moral life as the "ongoing endeavor of learning and being disciplined in the language of God," Paul J. Wadell offers the following thoughts:

> Learning to be moral is something like learning a language. A language is a system of communication that grows up around a common life. We talk to one another because there is something we want to share. In the same way, the Christian moral life is a system of communication that grows up around the core conviction that for us Jesus is Lord. If this is the most compelling fact of our lives, then it is something we want to understand, to live, and to share. The Christian moral life is nothing more than the ongoing endeavor to live from the good we call Jesus, a good that bonds us together and reminds us of who we want to be. This is why we can speak of Christian morality as a community's conversation about the purpose and goal of its life. To have a language is to have a way of life. To be a Christian is to be given the language of God that comes to us in Jesus and to embrace a way of life we call discipleship.

As we speak this language of God we are formed in it, and as we live it we become one with it. In this respect, the goal of the Christian moral life is to become articulate in the Word we call Jesus; in fact, so eloquently that we are his presence in the world.[13]

The liturgy promotes the Christian community's "conversation about the purpose and goal of its life" by promoting communal information, structuring communal formation, and promoting communal transformation.

The liturgy provides communal information by keeping biblical narratives at the forefront of the community's consciousness. At every liturgy, some portion of the Scriptures is proclaimed and at central liturgies (such as the Easter Vigil) the great sweep of biblical narrative is evoked. These narratives portray origins, development, and destiny in a way that shapes identity and gives purpose to worship participants. While various social, political, and ethnic groups will also cherish their own identity-conferring and -shaping narratives, the biblical narratives situate these limited narratives in an over-arching story about humanity's beginnings, history, and future. This religious narrative critiques and transcends individual communities' narratives, challenging racist and nationalist ideologies, while potentially immersing every human being in a common vision of life that grounds common values, virtues, and standards of behavior.

The liturgy models communal formation by symbolizing how the biblical tradition might be enacted in contemporary society. For example, the Kiss of Peace at Roman Rite Eucharistic worship, positioned after the Lord's Prayer and prior to the Fraction Rite, vividly demonstrates that right relationship with God (symbolized in eucharistic communion) necessarily involves the willingness to establish right relationship with other human beings. The "deformations" of this ritual gesture (from omitting it because it "intrudes" on personal preparation for communion to turning it into a frenzied search to enact one's affection for one's friends) defeat the purpose of the Rite: to embody the cost of communion for the disciples of the Lord Jesus, whose earthly ministry was marked by table fellowship with outcasts and the marginalized and whose cross-sacrifice is re-presented in the community's Eucharistic worship.

The liturgy encourages communal transformation by bringing the *status quo* under judgment and unleashing the Spirit-empowered imagination to envision new world structures under God's rule. Here the liturgy's sanctoral cycle is especially powerful. We do not honor the saints as quaint figures of nostalgia or as embodiments of abstract causes; rather we acknowledge our solidarity with the "cloud of witnesses" whose cooperation with God's grace transformed their world, praying that their influence might give us the courage to transform ours. Saints' lives (celebrated especially in the Office of Readings of the Liturgy of the Hours) give us models of how to denounce injustice when we encounter it and to commit ourselves to new ventures in incarnating faith from a variety of ages and cultures.

2. Critiquing Culture. Participating in liturgy critiques culture on at least three levels. Firstly, the very choice to celebrate liturgy, to "waste time with God" as a group, challenges society's claim to absolute power. By celebrating liturgy we proclaim that our deepest reality as humans is not something constructed and conferred solely by social, economic, or political systems. Sabbath as weekly and Pascha as yearly "festivals of freedom" have left their marks on Christian as well as Jewish worship.

Secondly, our ritual actions can fiercely confront "normal" patterns of social interaction. In a culture where some go hungry while others glut themselves, sharing the Eucharistic bread models a world where there is enough food for everyone and not too much for anyone. In a world where some drink only their tears while others dull consciousness through drunkenness, sharing the eucharistic cup models a world where all are welcome at sober festivity. In a world where children are sentimentalized or exploited, the liturgy honors them with perfumed oils, lit candles, and gleaming baptismal gowns. In a world where the sick are marginalized and hidden, the liturgy speaks their names, surrounds them with songs of hope, and touches them with healing massage. In a world where death is denied, the liturgy declares that it is only in and through death that true life is possible.

Thirdly, our ritual texts may directly name society's complicity with evil and challenge us to alternative action. While these prayers do not propose particular programs, they do specify Christian social action as the outgrowth of the Christian vision:

> God, you who have given to all peoples one origin and have willed that from all peoples a single family should gather together in yourself: fill the hearts of all with the ardor of your charity and ignite them with the desire of just progress for all their kindred; so that, through the goods that you have lavishly bestowed on all, the human personhood of each may be brought to perfection and that, with all division cast away, equality and justice might be established in human society...[Opening Prayer, Mass for the Progress of Peoples: *RM* 1970/1975].[14]

> God of peace, above all that peace that the violent spirit cannot capture and the bloody mind cannot receive, be present, so that those who are in harmony [with one another] might hold fast to the preservation of that good thing and those who are in discord [with one another] might be healed by the wiping out of every evil thing...[Opening Prayer, Other Prayers for Peace: *RM* 1970/1975].[15]

> God, whose Son deigned to take the form of a slave to redeem the human race from sin's slavery, grant to your servants cast into chains that they might be restored to the freedom that you have willed for all human beings, your children...[Opening Prayer, Mass for Those Unjustly Deprived of Liberty: *RM* 1970/1975].[16]

3. Celebrating Social Transformation. Social criticism is not the only stance the liturgy takes toward the world; it also names and celebrates instances where the world has been transformed under grace.

The liturgical homily provides an instance for celebrating social transformation. The homily is not a lecture on a given religious topic, though it must be informed by doctrine and may impart new knowledge about Church teaching. The homily is not a Scripture study lesson, although it is inspired by the Scriptures proclaimed and evokes their importance for the gathered worshipers. The homily is not a moralizing exhortation or a political pep rally, though it may profoundly engage social issues and invite believers to certain courses of action. Rather the liturgical homily is a "zone of truth-telling" where the preacher points to God's presence in contemporary Church and world and calls the gathered worshipers to praise and thanksgiving for God's action. At its best, the homily is just as forthright in identifying God's "amazing grace" operative in the world as it is in reproving a world that is not yet conformed to God's rule.

We noted above the liturgy's robust use of material elements as an embodiment of a theology of revelation in which God is manifest in the created order. It is equally important to note that most of the material elements employed in the liturgy are not used "raw" but have been altered by human industry. We do not offer wheat and grapes at eucharist, but bread ("that earth has given and human hands have made") and wine ("fruit of the vine and work of human hands"), elements already transformed by human labor to receive a further transformation in sacramental grace. We do not hallow olives and balsam at confirmation, but a perfumed oil confected by human ingenuity transformed by prayer to serve as the vehicle for God's anointing. The liturgy blesses and celebrates human creativity in the use of material creation, a creativity that does not exploit or destroy the created order but renders it useful for human purposes while adorning it with further beauty. (An ecological theology could be developed from reflection on how the liturgy stewards creation.)

Thirdly, ritual texts also celebrate God's ongoing interaction with the contemporary world. The Preface of Eucharistic Prayer II for Masses of Reconciliation is a premier instance of how divine activity in world-transformation can be imaged and celebrated in liturgical texts:

> Father, all-powerful and ever-living God, we praise and thank you through Jesus Christ our Lord for your presence and action in the world. In the midst of conflict and division, we know it is you who turn our minds to thoughts of peace. Your Spirit changes our hearts: enemies begin to

speak to one another, those who were estranged join hands in friendship, and nations see the way of peace together. Your Spirit is at work when understanding puts an end to strife, when hatred is quenched by mercy, and vengeance gives way to forgiveness. For this we should never cease to thank and praise you. We join with all the choirs of heaven as they sing forever to your glory.[17]

Conclusion

This chapter has sketched some of the ways in which participating in the liturgy assists worshipers to grow in right relationship with God, self, and others and reflecting on the liturgy assists spiritual and moral theology. By facilitating individuals' repeated encounters with the transcendent, solidarity with humanity, and ongoing religious development, the liturgy founds and fosters spirituality and spiritual theology. By promoting a common vision, critiquing culture, and celebrating social transformation the liturgy founds and fosters Christian action in the world and moral theology. In turn, spirituality and spiritual theology can unmask inauthenticity or confusion in the liturgy's symbolic manifestation of the encounter with God and protect it from any attempt to manipulate the divine. Christian living and moral theology can critique inadequacy or incoherence in the human relations modeled in liturgy and the behaviors promoted in its celebration.

My hope is that the future will reveal ever closer connections between liturgy, spirituality, and moral theology, that mystagogical reflection on what worshipers do, say, and mean will facilitate individual growth in holiness and communal transformation under grace until, having learned to live for others and the Other, we definitively enter God's reign:

There we hope to share in your glory when every tear will be wiped away. On that day we shall see you, our God, as you are. We shall become like you and praise you forever through Christ our Lord, from whom all good things come [Funeral embolism, Eucharistic Prayer III].[18]

SUGGESTED READING

Egan, John. "Liturgy and Justice: An Unfinished Agenda." *Origins* 13(1983): 399–411.

Empereur, James, and Christopher Kiesling. *The Liturgy That Does Justice: A New Approach to Liturgical Praxis.* Collegeville, Minn.: The Liturgical Press, 1991.

Fink, Peter E., ed. *The New Dictionary of Sacramental Worship.* Collegeville, Minn.: The Liturgical Press, 1990. S.v. "Liturgy and Christian Life" by Enda McDonagh; "Liturgy and Politics" by Walter J. Woods.

Grosz, Edward M., ed. *Liturgy and Social Justice.* Collegeville, Minn.: The Liturgical Press, 1989.

Haughey, John, ed.*The Faith That Does Justice.* New York: Paulist Press, 1977.

Hellwig, Monica. *Eucharist and the Hunger of the World.* New York: Paulist Press, 1976.

Henderson, J. Frank, Kathleen Quinn, and Stephen Larson. *Liturgy, Justice and the Reign of God: Integrating Vision and Practice.* New York: Paulist Press, 1989.

Hughes, Kathleen and Mark R. Francis, ed. *Living No Longer for Ourselves*: Collegeville, Minn.: The Liturgical Press, 1991.

Polish, Daniel and Eugene Fisher, ed.*Liturgical Foundations of Social Policy in the Catholic and Jewish Traditions.* Notre Dame, Ind.: University of Notre Dame Press, 1983.

Schmemann, Alexander. *For the Life of the World.* Crestwood, N.Y.: St. Vladimir's Seminary Press, 1977.

Schmidt, Herman and David Power, ed. *Politics and Liturgy.* Concilium, no. 92. New York: Herder and Herder, 1974.

Wainwright, Geoffrey. "Eucharist and/as Ethics." *Worship* 62 (1988): 123–37.

Warren, Michael. *Faith, Culture, and the Worshiping Community*: *Shaping the Practice of the Local Church.* New York: Paulist Press, 1989.

Chapter Six

Forming Right Relationships

KEVIN J. O'NEIL, C.SS.R.

All the enduring tales which capture the hearts of human beings treat, explicitly or implicitly, human relationships, matters of the heart. Whether one is recounting stories from the Book of Genesis or sorting through the great narratives of Greek mythology, whether one is deciphering medieval love letters or speeding through some racy contemporary novel, the tales which captivate us immerse us in comedy and tragedy, vows promised and broken, loves found and lost. They address the longing of the human heart and its fulfillment or failure, its love or its loss.

Throughout the ages, we have attempted to describe through literature and other art forms the bliss and anguish of successful and failed human relationships. The medieval Dominican friar Jordan of Saxony (1190–1237) captures in his letter to his friend, Diana d'Andolo, the joy which human relationships bring even when the friends are apart:

> You are so deeply engraven on my heart that the more I realize how truly you love me from the depths of your soul, the more incapable I am of forgetting you and the more constantly you are in my thoughts; for your love of me moves me deeply and makes my love for you burn more strongly.[1]

Contrast Jordan's words with those spoken by Muriel in the contemporary novel *The Company of Women* by Mary Gordon:

> My death will be a relief to everybody. There is nothing more lonely than to look among live faces for the face of one who will live after oneself and mourn, the face that, after one's death, will be changed by grief, and to find contempt or an undifferentiated kindness. I wait for a face to meet my face; I wait for the singular gaze, the gaze of permanent choosing, the glance of absolute preferment. This I have always waited for and never found, have hungered for and never tasted....I wait here to be looked upon with favor, to be chosen above others, knowing I will die the first beloved of no living soul.[2]

Muriel's words evoke sympathy, heartache, and sorrow for someone who has never felt love. They leave us with a sense of sadness that this particular human being missed out on something crucial for a good life.

My intention in this chapter is to examine the nature and scope of right relationships. I will begin in section one by focusing on the human person as relational, exploring why we even have to speak about right relationships at all. In the second section, I will look at friendship as the paradigm for right relationships. After reviewing two of the more significant ways in which friendship has been viewed in the Western philosophical tradition, I will argue that human friendship is indispensable for mature human development. In my final section, I will challenge the adequacy even of this conclusion and propose St. Thomas' understanding of friendship with God as the fundamental guarantor of all right relationships.

Relationality as Fundamental to Human Existence

A. Psychological Theories of Human Development. Why speak of right relationships at all? What is the context for our discussion about the convergence of the divine and the human in right relationships?

Psychological theories of human development depict growth as a progressive movement from self-absorption as an infant to the mature adult who has a clear self-identity and freely commits himself or herself to relationships with others. These include more personal relationships such as friendship and marriage, as well as an awareness of oneself as a member of the human community.[3] Erik Erikson, for example, speaks of various stages in a person's development (i.e., infancy, childhood, adolescence, young adulthood, middle adulthood, maturity), and a parallel series of concomitant tasks. The realization of tasks such as replacing mistrust with trust, shame and doubt with autonomy, role confusion with identity, isolation with intimacy, and the like, brings one toward human fulfillment. Notice the intrinsic relationality of these various tasks: one cannot trust or be intimate in isolation; we need others in our lives in order to grow and mature; without them, our autonomy and self-identity deconstruct. We regress into our baser instincts rather than transcend them. Erikson reflects the common practical wisdom of his profession when he concludes that the human condition is intrinsically relational.[4]

Critical to this development is the awareness of one's own nature as a relational being. Lack of this awareness presents immediate problems for the authentic realization of the person. Perhaps it is superfluous to state that lack of self-possession presumes ignorance of oneself as a relational being and that any attempt at associations with others will thereby be fatally flawed. Donald Evans accents this in his work, *Spirituality and Human Nature*.[5] In the chapter, "On Loving Oneself Well," he writes of the danger of what he terms "narcissechoism." This word merges the personality traits of two characters from classical Greek mythology, i.e., Narcissus and Echo, who function as archetypes of the modern dysfunctional personality. The former has an inflated image of himself, manipulates others to fall in love with him, and eventually falls in love with his own reflection in a pool. The latter is the victim of a curse that leaves her incapable of speaking for herself. She is condemned to repeat the last words of

what other people have said.[6] "Echo is the ultimate conformist....
Narcissus is the opposite, the epitome of self-inflation and self-
sufficiency."[7] Since they do not possess a firm grasp of who they
are, they are unable to enter into mature relationships with
others. Such are the risks facing individuals living in the
postmodern world.

Psychological theories of development, as well as reflection on
everyday experience, point to the nature of the human person as
relational and the need to foster relationships in order to become
complete human beings. If we fail to nurture sound human
relationships, we will never be anything more than mere fragile
shells of our deepest potential.

B. *Contemporary Theories of Moral Development.* If the general
psychological theories of human development insist on a
movement from self-absorption to self-transcendence, contemporary theories of moral development are even more explicit
about this type of growth in the moral life. Putting aside current
debates over a definitive theory of moral development, we can
safely conclude (since nearly all theories agree) that individuals
move through stages as they mature morally and develop a sense
of their own identity. This process of growth enables them to act
freely in the pursuit of internalized values, among them a sense
of belonging to and responsibility for others.[8]

Of course, not all the theorists agree on how this is done.
Lawrence Kohlberg, for example, expects a person to act morally
out of a sense of justice to others, moved ultimately by an
interiorization of the value of justice in one's own life.[9] He
proposes a theory of moral development whereby a person
progresses from an essentially self-centered morality, where one
acts in order to avoid punishment or to receive praise (pre-
conventional stage), to a morality performed to secure social
acceptability (conventional stage), to the internalization of values
and a sort of Kantian self-rule (post-conventional stage).
Kohlberg's principal early critic, Carol Gilligan, proposes instead
an "ethics of care" which likewise views moral maturity as
"other-directed."[10] Like the psychological theories of human
development treated earlier, both Kohlberg and Gilligan presume
that relationality is essential for successful moral development. It

is through relationships with others that a person matures and becomes most himself or herself. It is in these very relationships, when they are "appropriate" and "right," that one comes to a clearer understanding of one's own relational nature and continues to become aware of the close interdependence of the human community.

C. *Judeo-Christian Tradition.* The intrinsic relationality of the human person, while roundly supported in contemporary thought in the social sciences, also has firm justification within the Judeo-Christian tradition. This comes primarily from the doctrine of the Trinity and from the theology of creation, which posits that we are made in the image of God.

1. *The Doctrine of the Trinity.* The Triune God manifests to humanity a divine community. As theologians have attempted to describe the precise correlation among the persons of the Trinity over the centuries, they have taken for granted their fundamentally relational nature.[11] One of the more explicit examples of this comes from the twelfth-century Victorine author, Richard of St. Victor, who speaks of the Father as Lover, the Son as Beloved, and the Spirit as Love itself.[12] Regardless of the precise theory of relationships one espouses with regard to Trinitarian life, one always finds a mutual giving and receiving among the three persons. The Trinity, one might say, reveals God to us as "pure self-gift."[13] Pope John Paul II affirms this perception in his encyclical on the Holy Spirit. He writes: "...in the Holy Spirit the intimate life of the Triune God becomes totally gift, an exchange of mutual love between the Divine Persons, and that through the Holy Spirit God exists in the mode of gift. It is the Holy Spirit who is the personal expression of this self-giving, of this being-love."[14]

For our purposes, the nature of the Trinity is significant because of our belief, founded in the Book of Genesis, that the human person is created in God's own image and likeness (cf. Gn 1:26). This foundational and revelatory point concerning the nature of the human person propels us to examine who this God is in whose image we are made. It is in the very nature of God that we find the basis for the affirmation of the Christian anthropology that "being a human being involves other human beings."[15]

2. *The Image and Likeness of God.* The identity of the God in whose image we have been made is clarified in other books of the Scriptures. Gian Carlo Vendrame points out that "the central and constitutive thread of revelation is of a personalist and communitarian nature: what the Bible illustrates is the covenant of God with the chosen people which is developed historically in the faithful self-donation of God and in the formation of God's people in the world."[16] The Scriptures present a relational God, a God who is "pure self-gift." Attention to the stories of Israel and of Jesus point to a God desirous of being in relationship with creation.

a. Old Testament. The image of God that we come to know in the Old Testament is that of a God who is madly in love with his people. The God of Exodus is the one who joins a people to himself. In the Book of Leviticus we read: "I will be your God and you will be my people" (Lv 26:12). The God who took on the role of the 'next of kin' in liberating the Israelites from slavery in Egypt not only sets them up in a relationship with himself, but also with one another. He speaks of them as his people. Similarly, in the prophetic literature we see the image of God as the faithful spouse. "I will espouse you forever: I will espouse you in right and in justice, in love and in mercy" (Ho 2:21). The Wisdom literature, moreover, presents God's relationship to Israel as that of a lover to his beloved (cf. The Song of Songs). Even these few examples show that the God of the Old Testament would clearly go to any lengths to stay in relationship with the people whom he has called his own. One author has remarked that "God's salvific initiative toward the people is prior to any human effort rising to know and love God, and it surpasses its possibilities and limits."[17]

b. New Testament. New Testament literature states repeatedly that the image of the relational God in whose likeness we have been made is seen in the person of Jesus Christ, the image of the Invisible God (Col 1:15).[18] The Letter to the Hebrews states in chapter one: "In times past, God spoke in fragmentary and varied ways to our fathers through the prophets; in this, the final age, he has spoken to us through his Son....This Son is the reflection of the Father's glory, the exact representation of the Father's being" (Heb 1:1–3). In the person of Jesus Christ we have both the fullest revelation of who God is, the God in whose image we have been made, but also the paradigm for humanity. He is "the archetypal Christ, God's 'definition' of what humanity and the world are all about."[19] In the person of Jesus Christ human beings find the image of God and their own destiny most fully revealed, precisely because he is both God *and* human.

If, as we discussed above, the task of psychological and moral development is to move steadily toward a greater understanding of who one is in relation to self and others, identified as a movement from self-absorption to self-transcendence, so too is this the case for the Church's theological reflection. Because we are made in the image and likeness of God, we reach our full potential only in relationship as generous, self-giving people.

Friendship: The Paradigm for Right Relationships

Thus far, I have merely tried to answer the question, "why speak of right relationships at all?" As we have seen, modern psychology, theories of moral development, even Christian theology tell us that human fulfillment comes only through forming right relationships. I would now like to suggest that the paradigm for right relationships is friendship. By this I mean that people reach their fullest potential not by focusing on themselves and their own needs, but by becoming friends, by moving from self-absorption to self-transcendence in genuine care for each other. Friendship is the appropriate context for right relationships, regardless of from what theoretical context one is speaking. In true friendship, there exists the condition for the possibility of a genuine meeting of the divine and the human.

A. Friendship in Classical Western Philosophy. Gilbert Meilander has written that it is not too gross an exaggeration to say that all Western thought on the nature of friendship is a series of footnotes to Plato and Aristotle.[20] In them, we have what many consider the two most important theories of friendship from classical writings. For this reason, a brief presentation of Plato's and Aristotle's views on the significance of friendship for the moral life will contribute immensely to our discussion. My intention here is not to provide a detailed account of these two philosophers on this point, but only to draw an adequate backdrop for my own line of argumentation.

    1. Friendship in Plato (c. 427–327 B.C.). Plato's thinking on *philia*, the love characteristic of friendship, appears chiefly in the Socratic dialogue, *Lysis* (c. 370 B.C.), and to a lesser extent in the *Phaedrus*, and in the *Symposium*. In his opinion, people seek out beauty as they see it in others because they are moved by *eros*, an inner passion of divine origin. The beauty that they discover in their friend, however, should move them instead to an appreciation of the true beauty that lies beyond the visible world. For Plato, who thought the soul was imprisoned in a body and thus subject to the limitations of the visible world, humanity has the task of going beyond the confines of this earth and to get in touch once again with its original state beyond the limits of matter. One's experience of beauty on earth causes one to "remember" true beauty in the other world. Plato, one might say, sees the imperfection of all earthly existence and then encourages us to find perfection by contemplating the archetypal Ideas of the eternal realm.

    How does this affect Plato's understanding of friendship? He certainly recognizes that we are drawn to others in friendship. Our friends, however, are meant to lead us beyond themselves to an appreciation of "true beauty" (inasmuch as we can grasp it). Plato would look down upon our tendency to want to savor any tangible relationship of friendship. In such situations, he would say that we are being driven completely by *eros* and not moving toward *philia* which is characterized by a profound love of wisdom itself. For this reason, friendship, for Plato, is neither particular nor exclusive. Friends do not "cling to one another," but help each other in the pursuit of true beauty. There is an obvious quality of instrumentality to the idea of friendship in Plato's thought. Friendship is a means to an end. We are encouraged to seek out anyone who can assist us to get in closer contact with true beauty. As Meilander notes: "Such a love is not exclusive but is potentially universal in scope."[21]

    2. Friendship in Aristotle (384–322 B.C.). Plato's pupil, Aristotle, takes a different tack. He identifies three types of friendship:

those of pleasure, those of utility, and those of virtue. In the case of the first two, he notes that people sometimes become "friends" because of the pleasure or advantage they incur. In such relationships, there is little genuine affection for the other person's own sake; the object of friendship is not the goodness of the other person, but the resulting personal gain. For Aristotle, these self-serving relationships are friendships only in a secondary sense.

True friendships, by way of contrast, are marked by an attraction to the good that is embodied in the other and a desire for the other's continued well-being. Aristotle writes:

> Only the friendship of those who are good and similar in their goodness is perfect. For these people each alike wish good for the other *qua* good, and they are good in themselves. And it is those who desire the good of their friends for the friends' sake that are most truly friends, because each loves the other for what he is, and not for any incidental quality. Accordingly, the friendship of such men lasts so long as they remain good; and goodness is an enduring quality.[22]

For Aristotle, a true friendship is particular by its very nature; it will always indicate a preferential love for this or that individual. This type of friendship has a formative effect on those in the relationship. Attracted to the good existing in them, friends nurture virtues in their own lives in order to continue to pursue the good in its many forms.

When treating Plato, I noted that friendship serves as a means to a greater end; it moves beyond one's friend to a contemplation of higher things. If friendship in Plato moves from the particular to the universal, in Aristotle one finds the exact reverse. A person moves from a general concern of good will for all people to a more specific demonstration of it in friendship. For Aristotle, this notion of friendship has the twofold effect of promoting both the goodness in the friends involved in the relationship and the goodness of society as a whole.

There are, of course, some common elements to both Plato's and Aristotle's presentations. Both presume self-transcendence on the part of the person pursuing friendship. Whether one sees friendship as a means to reaching Wisdom or as a recognition of another's goodness and a desire to promote that goodness, the activity is "other-directed." Both Plato and Aristotle, moreover, assert that attraction to goodness moves a person to seek out others in friendship.

B. *The Significance of Friendship for the Moral Life.* The effect of friendship on the individuals themselves is also critical to our reflection. Why should friendship be qualified as the paradigm for "right relationships"? Why should its essential characteristics of benevolence, reciprocity, and mutual indwelling be so important for authentic human growth and development? Understood in the Aristotelian sense, true friendships enable a person to open up and to extend himself or herself in pursuit of the good. In friendship, a person sharpens his or her own perception of the good and recognizes its embodiment in the person and actions of another. This process disposes one to and confirms one in a virtuous life where one's own attitudes and actions reflect the good. If human maturity is characterized by self-transcendence, if progress in moral development is marked by interiorization of values and genuine care for others, if spiritual growth is signalled by conformity to the image of God, a God who is "pure self-gift," then true friendship among human beings clearly nurtures development on the psychological, moral and spiritual dimensions of human existence and promotes the fulfillment of the human being in the process. In the words of Paul Wadell, "Friendship begins in recognition of the other, requires appreciation for them precisely as other, and deepens as each moves further out of self and toward the other. In this respect, friendship is a paradigm for moral growth."[23]

Friendship with God

But are human relationships enough? If we speak of full human maturity, superior moral development, conformity to the image of God, are these to be attained through human relationships alone? Can one reach full human goodness solely through human friendships?

St. Augustine (354–430) thinks not. Writing in his *Confessions*, he seriously ponders the death of his closest friend:

> I marveled that other men should live, because he, whom I had loved as if he would never die, was dead. I marveled more that I, his second self, could live when he was dead. Well has someone said of his friend that he is half of his soul. For I thought that my soul and his soul were but one soul in two bodies. Therefore, my life was a horror to me, because I would not live but as a half.[24]

Powerful words from Augustine. Yet it is precisely this experience which prompts his reflection on the nature of friendship and the place of God in human friendships. Augustine, who says "our hearts are restless until they rest in Thee, O God," realizes that he has rested his heart in his friend. He does not regret ever having loved his friend, but only that he loved his friend "as though he were one who would never die."[25] He interprets his friend's death as a stark reminder that we should praise beauty and goodness as we see it in one another but that our friendships should be in God and lead us to God. Later in the Confessions he writes:

> If you find pleasure in bodily things, praise God for them, and direct your love to their maker, lest because of things that please you, you may displease him. If you find pleasure in souls, let them be loved in God. In themselves they are but shifting things; in him they stand firm; else they would pass and perish. In him, therefore, let them be loved....He did not make all things and then leave them, but they are from him and in him.[26]

Like Plato, Augustine realizes that attachment to one's friend must be transformed. No single person can ever fully embody the ideal of Beauty or Wisdom. Friends merely hint at it; they are only pale shadows of the ideal. True to form, Augustine follows and "Christianizes" Plato in proposing that "the love of friendship is a sign and a call intended to draw the friends on toward love of God."[27]

Augustine recognizes that anyone who is caught up in another's goodness, as he was with his friend, cannot find complete, absolute human fulfillment without somehow allowing God into the picture. Earlier in book four, he writes:

> For whatever way the soul of man turns, it is fixed upon sorrows any place except in you, even though it is fixed upon beautiful things that are outside of you and outside itself. Yet these beauteous things would not be at all, unless they came from you.[28]

As good and beautiful as the relationship of friendship is, as fulfilling as the recognition and enjoyment of beauty in this world is, it is nonetheless incomplete in the face of the One who is all Good, all Beauty, all Wisdom. All of humanity is limited and reflects wonderfully yet inadequately the fullness of the Creator. This ought not lead to a depreciation of the value of particular friendships, but to an awareness of their importance. Without them, no one could ever enter into an intimate relationship of friendship with God.

To illustrate this point, Augustine uses the example of speech and understanding. Although we would like to understand everything, knowledge normally comes to us through words which must be formulated, uttered, heard, interpreted—and which, ultimately, come and go.[29] We would like to comprehend all things, but we must be content with grasping what is made known to us through speech. Because of our own limitedness, we are forced to deal with particulars. So it is with the goodness encountered in friends. In the words of Adele Fiske: "The friend is not lost in the Absolute, nor left behind as a step in the ascent, but is a permanent revelation of God, a necessary complement to the soul in its movement to God."[30] Through a conscious relationship with God as well as with human beings, we are capable of finding and reaching fulfillment.

Centuries later, Augustine's insight would be further elaborated by St. Thomas Aquinas (1225–74). Writing about growth in the virtuous life, he remarks that a person's appreciation and grasp of the good comes in stages.[31] He enumerates three in particular for a person's perfection in charity or, as it is otherwise understood, advancement in "a certain friendship" with God. The first consists largely in turning from evil and avoiding sin; the second, in the daily struggle to preserve the virtuous life. In the light of my previous remarks, human friendship arises in this context as an important *sine qua non* for anyone wishing to lead such a life. The final stage is to apply oneself "chiefly to the work of cleaving to God and enjoying him, which is characteristic of the perfect who *long to depart and to be with Christ.*"[32] Only in this way will we grow in charity, the form of all other virtues. Only through friendship with God can we come into contact with our original destiny, our original image and likeness, our fulfillment. In an earlier question Thomas writes:

> An excellence obviously increases as the first and unique source of the excellence is approached—somewhat as the brightness of a lighted object increases as it approaches the source of light. A deficiency increases, however, not with proximity to, but with distance from, what is perfect and supreme: that is precisely what makes a thing defective.[33]

Only when friendship opens itself to a relationship with God can it satisfy the human spirit and move the human heart to absolute fulfillment. In this respect, friendship with God is the definitive right relationship for human beings.

Conclusion

To say much more would go beyond prescribed boundaries of our task. I have attempted in this chapter to do three things. In the first place, I examined the nature of the human person by investigating material from human psychology, moral development, and Christian theology. I noted here that the human person is a relational being by nature, someone who reaches perfection by moving from self-absorption to self-transcendence. In the second place, I proposed that friendship is the appropriate framework for speaking about right relationships among human beings. At this point, I showed that true friendship orients a person toward the good embodied in another human being and helps him or her to seek the other's good in an atmosphere of genuine care and reciprocal concern. Finally, I pointed out that although friendship is indeed beneficial to both parties involved, there is limited access to the good due to the intrinsic limitations of the human condition. Here, I argued that, even though human relationships are an essential part in one's development in the moral life, they are not sufficient in and of themselves.

What are we to conclude from all of this? Far from pulling people away from human friendship, friendship with God graces human beings to live virtuous lives even in the face of their limitations. This graced relationship with the One who is all Good, all True, all Beautiful, the One in whose image and likeness we have been made, breaks through our human restrictions on goodness and allows for new and creative possibilities for loving relationships. If true friendship encourages friends to make the cares of their friends their own, then our possibilities for self-gift and, consequently, self-perfection are limitless when those same friendships are touched by the divine. In the end, right relationships are formed wherever God and human meet. Such is the journey all of us travel through life, the destiny toward which we strive and hope one day fully to attain.

SUGGESTED READING

Aelred of Rievaulx. *Spiritual Friendship*. Translated by Mary Eugenia Laker. Cistercian Series, no. 5. Kalamazoo, Mich.: Cistercian Publications, 1974.

Aristotle. *The Ethics of Aristotle: Nichomachean Ethics*. Translated by J. A. K. Thomson. Revised by Hugh Tredennick. With an Introduction and Bibliography by Jonathan Barnes. New York: Penguin Books, 1976.

Augustine of Hippo. *The Confessions of St. Augustine*. Translated by John K. Ryan. Garden City, N.Y.: Image Books, 1960 (esp. bk. 4, chaps. 4–15 ; bk. 6).

Evans, Donald. *Spirituality and Human Nature*. Albany: State University of New York Press, 1993.

Fiores, Stefano de and Tullo Gioffi, eds. *Nuevo Diccionario de Espirituaidad*. Translated by Augusto Guerra. Madrid: Ediciones Paulinas, 1983. S.v. "Horizontalismo /verticalismo," by Gian Carlo Vendrame.

Helminiak, Daniel A. *Spiritual Development: An Interdisciplinary Study*. Chicago: Loyola University Press, 1987.

Meilaender, Gilbert. *Friendship: A Study in Theological Ethics*. Notre Dame, Ind.: University of Notre Dame Press, 1981.

Pakaluk, Michael, ed. *Other Selves: Philosophers on Friendship*. Indianapolis, Ind./ Cambridge: Hackett Publishing Co., 1991.

Shelton, Charles M. *Morality of the Heart: A Psychology for the Christian Moral Life*. New York: Crossroad, 1990.

Wadell, Paul J. *Friendship and the Moral Life*. Notre Dame, Ind.: University of Notre Dame Press, 1989.

————.*The Primacy of Love*. New York/Mahwah, N.J.: Paulist Press, 1992.

Chapter Seven

Docility to the Spirit: Discerning the Extraordinary in the Ordinary

HERBERT ALPHONSO, S.J.

Contemporary man, contemporary woman yearn for integrated living. They are loath to tolerate any dichotomy or divorce
between faith and life. It is, they tell us, the very texture of
their daily existence—the prosaically simple, commonplace,
ordinary—that must become more and more the warp and woof
of the kingdom of God. They insist that they do not need to
escape from their daily tasks, their human contacts, their secular
responsibilities in order to find God or sanctify themselves.
Indeed, it is at the very heart of their earthly tasks, their human
contacts, their secular responsibilities that they are to encounter
the living God and there enter into personal dialogue and
communion with him. For, in keeping with the contemporary
theology of earthly realities and human values, which pervades
Vatican II's "Pastoral Constitution on the Church in the Modern
World,"[1] all reality is shot through with the presence and activity
of God—or, as a Teilhard de Chardin would say, all reality is "le
milieu divin."[2]

This "spirituality of the incarnation," as it is called, this
"Christianity in the market-place" is the very core of that
apostolic spirituality which today, in many writings on spirituality in general and on prayer in particular, is being termed

112

"contemplation in action"[3] or, more existentially, "finding God in all things."[4] It is no secret that the whole range of apostolic spirituality must address itself, first and last, to the radical problem of the apostolic vocation—namely, to its living unity and integration which, in real experience, is always threatened to be sundered and torn apart by the apparently conflicting demands of contemplation and action, prayer and active apostolate, faith and life. It is quite remarkable, in fact, that ever since Vatican II all the documents of the Church on apostolic spirituality—be they addressed to priests, or to apostolic religious, or to the laity[5]—have been insistently calling Christian apostles to this *living unity and integration* which is the heart of the apostolic vocation and life.

The Christian Spiritual Life: Its Unity and Growth

The image of the growing and maturing spiritual life is not that of the human person who by a promethean Pelagian, or at best semi-Pelagian, effort struggles up toward God. It is, as biblical revelation so powerfully and insistently inculcates, God who comes to us, who ceaselessly comes to the human person in other persons, events and circumstances of time, place, and action: "He comes, comes, ever comes."[6] It is not God who is short-handed; it is we, human beings, who are not ready or "free"—or, as masters of the spiritual life such as Ignatius Loyola would love to say, "disposed"—for the God who is always coming into our lives, enslaved as we are from within by our likes and dislikes, our attachments and repugnances, our prejudices and inhibitions, our self-love, self-will, and self-interest.

And so, the authentic Christian image of the growing, maturing spiritual life is that of man and woman who, under the action of the ever-coming God (for the primacy and initiative belong to God), must become more and more free, that is, must actively allow God to *free them progressively from* all those barriers that block the invading love and life and power of God, in order to become more and more *free for* God, more and more docile and available to God's presence and action in them.[7] "Active receptivity," then, is at the heart of the Christian spiritual life.

In this light, therefore, growth toward Christian perfection and its unity lies in the *subjective experiential process of growth in inner freedom*—in both dimensions of growing "freedom from" and of progressive "freedom for," which latter is rightly termed "docility" or availability. This docility or availability or active receptivity entails increasing openness to the Holy Spirit; it means awareness of his presence and activity in and around us in order to back it up, second, and support it. This openness or docility to the Spirit is the heart of all true and deepening union with God: for the Spirit leads us by his gifts; through these gifts, he urges us to those active purifications and accomplishes in us those passive purifications, which are so necessary for profound union with God and all true sanctity.

It is possible, then, to find God, to have a day of profound union with God, to have a day of profound "prayer" in the midst of absorbing activity—we mean not just the "exercise" of prayer, but the "spirit" of prayer which is that basic thrust and attitude of life that we have called "growing inner freedom." For union with God is not, in the first instance and above all, to be placed in the quiet and repose of the "exercise" of prayer—how could it be, if prayer itself, which takes place in the heart, requires that the heart be interiorly free? Nor is union with God to be preserved in the midst of absorbing activity, as we were often taught, principally by some artificial exercise of the presence of God, by aspirations or ejaculatory prayers or some such spiritual "sleight-of-hand" and stratagem—how, if activity often requires the whole person who cannot be psychologically divided, except of course at the risk of very successfully creating a kind of spiritual schizophrenia? The secret of "prayer" and union with God at the heart of absorbing activity is to be found in the incessant denial and dispossession of self, with true interior freedom, in the very thing in hand at every moment—a self-dispossession that makes one free, open, "docile" to the God who perpetually comes. St. John of the Cross was once asked a very curious question by his brothers. "Fray Juan," they said, "how do you enter into ecstasy?" His answer: "By obeying!" Not obedience merely to the orders of superiors, he went on to explain, but the obedience of all times and all moments—that ceaseless dispossession of self that makes us docile and pliable, yes, to the orders of superiors, but also to events, things and persons as they come along: to failure and success, to health and sickness, to difficult and easy human relations—in a word, free for and open to the God who comes ceaselessly into our lives to redeem and transform them.

Contemporary Relevance of Ignatian Pedagogy

As a student of St. Ignatius' school of spirituality, I have often asked myself why it speaks so eloquently to the men and women of today. I have had occasion to experience this lively, even enthusiastic, interest in Ignatian pedagogy during my twelve years as Director of the "Ignatian Spirituality Centre" at Jesuit Headquarters. Today I think I can say with more than sufficient evidence that this is principally because Ignatian pedagogy, such as it is spelled out in "The Spiritual Exercises of St. Ignatius," leads precisely to that unified integration of contemplation and action, of prayer and active apostolate, of faith and life that contemporary man and woman so thirst for.

Not in theory, but in the school of his own experience guided by the Lord,[8] Ignatius learned that it is the same spiritual perfection, which permits at one and the same time prayer and activity, that unites with God and sanctifies. In other words, what Ignatius assimilated in the crucible of experience was that the integration or solution of the tension that we experience between contemplation and action, or faith and life, lies neither in the "exercise" of prayer as such nor in the "exercise" of activity as such, but in *what is typical of Christian spiritual perfection* at the basis of both prayer and activity, both faith and life. This typical element we have seen above is "inner freedom," or docility or availability to the Spirit. This it is that makes prayer true prayer, and activity true activity; so, this it is that integrates all of life, making of everyday simple, commonplace, ordinary life true "prayer"—that is, authentic union with God. And this, not on the abstract level of neat theory as it were, but, as we have seen, as a

subjective experiential process of spiritual growth and maturing—
namely, a personal formation, training, pedagogy. Precisely this
is the entire book of the Exercises of St. Ignatius, their inner
dynamics, as we are terming it today.[9]

The Dynamics of the Ignatian Exercises

The starting point of the Exercises is that initial in-depth
attitude of the exercitant's total readiness for God from where he
or she existentially is "to enter upon them with magnanimity and
generosity toward their Creator and Lord, offering Him their
entire will and liberty, that His Divine Majesty may dispose of
them and all they possess according to His most holy will" (*Spir.
Exercises*, 5)—which is nothing but the *Principle and Foundation* of
the Exercises. Working on this initial attitude of "freedom from"
and "freedom for," Ignatius takes his exercitant through a
pedagogical process of deepening inner freedom. Through the
exercitant's commitment to a profound and prolonged praying
experience on the objective normative process of salvation
history, he submits the person of the exercitant actively to God's
freeing action: first, on the obvious plane of sin, imperfection, and
disorder (First Week meditations); then, more deeply on the level
of the exercitant's values, value systems and criteria of living
(Second Week contemplations of the mysteries of Christ, in which
Christ's criteria, standards, and values constitute a challenge to
those of the exercitant impelling him or her to put on those of
Christ); indeed, this active submission of the exercitant to God's
freeing action is pursued finally on the deepest existential level of
the subtle securities of life so very jealously shielded and guarded
by the exercitant—to start with, the securities in the obscured
recesses of the intellect (*Two Standards* meditation), then those
residing in the subtle motivations of the will (*Three Classes*
meditation), and finally those lodged in the hidden folds of the
heart (*Three Kinds of Humility* consideration).

Existentially freed thus on the deepest and subtlest levels, the
exercitant is now *free for* God, free "to seek and find the will of
God in the disposition of his or her life for the salvation of his or

her soul" (*Spir. Exercises*, 1). What Ignatius terms "elección" therefore—election or choice or decision—is, at its heart, a becoming aware in deepening inner freedom of God's personal plan or design or will for the exercitant, in order that he or she may, through the process of confirmation carried out in the Third and Fourth Weeks of the Exercises, accept it profoundly in his or her life to live it out faithfully and generously. In this perspective, that categorical Ignatian sentence, tucked away in a corner of the book of the Exercises at the end of the "Election" documents, becomes the key to the entire dynamics of the Exercises: "Let everyone keep in mind that in all things that concern the spiritual life progress is in proportion to getting out of self-love, self-will, and self-interest" (*Spir. Exercises*, 189)—in other words, a process and dynamic movement of growing, deepening inner freedom.

Consequently this, and this alone, is the process by which Ignatius prepares his exercitant for that final "Contemplation To Attain Love," which is not one more exercise—the last one—of the book of the Exercises, but a new way of praying: as Ignatius says, "so that...I may *in all things* love and serve the Divine Majesty" (*Spir. Exercises*, 233)—finding God in all things, loving him in all creatures and all creatures in him, that is *the prayer of everyday life*, or, better still, *praying the very texture of everyday life*: DISCERNING THE EXTRAORDINARY IN THE ORDINARY.

What thus stands out in bold relief in the progressive dynamics of the Exercises is that the initial attitude of the exercitant's freedom in letting go totally into God's hands from where he or she existentially is at the beginning of the Exercises—his or her initial "docility" (cf. *Spir. Exercises*, 5)—has been increasingly deepened through a spiralling experiential process of growing inner freedom till it has *itself* become, in the "Contemplation To Attain Love," an interiorized, assimilated and consolidated attitude for life: *free now to find God in all things, free now to pray always*. In concrete terms, it is amazing to note that the very same initial "magnanimity and generosity...offering Him their entire will and liberty, that His Divine Majesty may dispose of them and all they possess according to His most holy will" (*Spir. Exercises*, 5), which is what the *Principle and Foundation* (cf. *Spir. Exercises*, 23) really is, is literally echoed, almost word for word, at the final level of spiral deepening in the "Take, Lord, and receive all my liberty, my memory, my understanding, and my entire will, all that I have and possess...dispose of it wholly according to your will" (*Spir. Exercises*, 234) of the "Contemplation To Attain Love."

One might well affirm, then, that there are two summits in the Exercises: the *Election* and the *Contemplation To Attain Love*. But these are not two different summits: they are one and the same summit looked at from two different angles. The *Election* is, in its deepest sense,[10] the exercitant's most intimately personal and unique way of being and living free of self—free of the "self-love, self-will and self-interest" of which Ignatius speaks at the end of the Election documents (cf. *Spir. Exercises*, 189). The *Election* is, in other words, the exercitant's most intimately personal and unique way of being and living wholly free for God and totally "docile" or available to him, thus finding him in all things, loving him in all creatures and all creatures in him—which is the grace of the *Contemplation To Attain Love*: "...I may in all things love and serve" ("en todo amar y servir": *Spir. Exercises*, 233). For, no differently from St. John of the Cross, Ignatius Loyola is deeply convinced that the summits of detachment from self or of inner freedom are themselves the summits of love. Speaking symbolically, Mount Carmel and Mount Tabor—the summit of detachment ("nada, nada"[11]) and the summit of love ("en todo amar") respectively—are one and the same summit. For in the heart that is interiorly free, open, "docile" and available, the Lord pours out the rich abundance of his love, pours out and gives *himself*.

The Crying Need for Discernment, Even Daily Discernment

With all this said, however, one could be plagued with a sort of nagging question. It is all very well to show, and even most heartily to acknowledge, that Ignatius Loyola *effectively* leads his exercitant through the very inner dynamics of his Exercises to the point of "finding God in all things," to truly discerning the extraordinary in the ordinary. The question is: how in practice is this attitude of "docility to the Spirit," this basic thrust of life, this "spirit of prayer" to be preserved and maintained in the midst of the hustle and bustle and the hectic round of everyday living? Here, too, Ignatius reveals himself as the master pedagogue: his teaching and insistence on the daily "Examen of Conscience"— or, as we are rightly terming it today, the "Consciousness Examen"—is nothing but the practical pedagogy of effectively reaching "inner freedom" in the crucible of real everyday experience. It is, in very truth, the whole dynamics of the Exercises recapitulated, gone through and lived out at the heart of real daily life. In this context, it is not surprising to learn that Ignatius would say to the Minister of the Professed House in Rome: "Father so-and-so is ill; you may dispense or excuse him from making his period of personal prayer, not however from his examen of conscience."[12] Is this an index of a sort of morbid spirituality? Or is it, rather, Ignatius' lively consciousness of the need to work for inner freedom through the real experience of illness, so as to "find God" in that very illness? Today we have become intensely alive to the fact that the Ignatian examen of conscience (= consciousness examen), far from being an exercise of mere morality, is in fact the daily exercise of spiritual discernment.[13] And life today—the very real world of today, the very real Church of today—stands sorely in need of spiritual discernment.

The world is in the throes of radical change, phenomenal change, explosive change. In a vertiginously fast-moving world, which in the course of eighty to eighty-five years has stridden rapidly from atomic and nuclear to jet and space age, which in the last few years has seen well-entrenched regimes fall, iron curtains rift and carefully-constructed walls crumble, is it too much to venture the statement that *the* chief characteristic of our age has been, and is, "change"? But sudden, accelerated change means an explosive upheaval of values; and in an explosive upheaval of values we, human beings, are prone to take up extreme positions. Either, feeling threatened by the phenomenal pace and rate of change, we hold on for dear life, with tenacious obstinancy, to the "traditional" values and "absolute security" of the past—and then condemn ourselves to sterile fossilization; or, intoxicated by the heady wine of novelty, we discard with one sweeping revolutionary stroke all that is "traditional" and of the past, in the belief and proclamation of a "brave new world," an absolutely new age, something "new" every day and every moment of every day—only to wake up one day to find that our brave new world has gone up in smoke, the smoke of utopian dreams, because we had thrown out the baby with the bath water! "Old" and "new," "traditional" and "modern," or for that matter "conservative" and "progressive"—these are certainly not the criteria to decide what is true and what is good. For these criteria we must look elsewhere: to the mind and the spirit, the teaching and the life of Jesus Christ, who is himself goodness and truth. If there is one virtue, then, that our age of confusion and upheaval of values is direly in need of, it is *discernment*; for this world of ours, the exhortation of Paul to the Thessalonians some two thousand years ago is as actual as ever: "Do not stifle the Spirit. Do not despise prophecies. Test (*'dokimazete'* =discern) everything; retain what is good" (1 Th 5:19–21).

And the Church—what about the Church? Inserted as she is into human history, the Church has not escaped—cannot escape—the stamp of the times. The Second Vatican Council constituted for the Church a major breakthrough of the Spirit in our times: not without foundation has it been characterized as a "new Pentecost," making the post-conciliar years, like the first ages of Christianity, a time of ferment and challenge—a time when the Spirit of God, who makes all things new, is blowing freely, fully, furiously. Witness, for instance, the extraordinary burgeoning of vital spiritual and religious movements like the Charismatic Renewal, the Focolarini, the Neo-Catechumenate Movement, Basic Christian Communities, to mention only a few. But, if we know anything of the spiritual world, it is precisely when the Spirit of God is blowing freely, fully, furiously that the counter-spirits are equally furiously at work,[14] generating an experience of massive confusion and an upheaval of values. It is a matter of daily experience, if we are in close pastoral contact with our people, to come up against the anguished earnestness with which, in an atmosphere charged with competing doctrines and systematically eroding moral values, they plead with us: "Do tell us, we beg you, what is true and what is false, what is right and what is wrong. So many things are being trumpeted on one side and the other, and all this by seemingly responsible persons, that we no longer know where we stand." Now, if in such a situation, the Church would by no means want "to snuff out the Spirit," yet at the same time not want "to be carried away by every spirit," then she stands in crying need of spiritual discernment in all her members—in her hierarchy, her priests and religious, her committed laity, in every one of her states of life and spheres of living. So central is spiritual discernment to the living out of Christianity today, that it is insistently being said that Christian formation today is to be basically and radically a formation to discernment.

At this precise point, then, is the Ignatian "examen of consciousness"—the daily exercise of discernment—being increasingly recognized as of primordial and capital significance in the world and the Church of today—concretely, in the existential realistic everyday life of the men and women of today. For, as we have hinted earlier on, this "consciousness examen" is the recapitulation, at the heart of everyday experience, of the very same pedagogy and dynamics of "inner freedom" as is spelled out at length in the book of the Exercises. Little wonder that it results, as does the process of the Exercises itself, in that "finding God in all things" which is the ceaseless prayer of everyday life—that "docility to the Spirit" which ceaselessly discerns the extraordinary in the ordinary.

The Consciousness Examen[15]

How and in what sense—briefly, at any rate—is the "consciousness examen" the concentrated summing-up of the whole dynamics of the Exercises?

If we are to do a typically *Christian* exercise of discernment, we must begin with "thanksgiving"—namely, the acknowledgment that it is God who has been coming into our lives, that the primacy and initiative belong to him who, in all our experience of the day, has been coming to us with his gifts, his grace, his life and love. We may not have recognized or "discerned" his presence and action; he was nonetheless actively coming to us in all that experience. We *thank* him; we are now *actively receptive* to him and his saving action. This, in effect, is our principle and foundation.

Within this specifically Christian context, we start our exercise of discernment. We know that what is distinctive of Christian discernment is that it is based on *experience*. Not because we marshal the reasons for something, then the reasons against it, weigh up and ponder these reasons, and finally plump for the side that carries the weightier reasons, have we been doing discernment. That may well be a prudential process. Authentic discernment is done by sifting through *inner experience*; this, in New Testament language, is what is termed "discernment of spirits."[16] And so, we pick up our real *experience* of the day, whatever be that experience, positive or negative. If we are to deal with this experience, to reach true "inner freedom" through it, we can do so only by first becoming *conscious* of our experience (hence "examen of consciousness"), then *accepting* it for what it is. "Acceptance" is *not* the same as "approval"; "approval" or "disapproval" is a *judgment*, "acceptance" or "non-acceptance" is an *attitude*. God cannot "approve" of so many things we say and do, yet in the very same things he "accepts" us *unconditionally*—— of this the Gospel of Jesus Christ is a relentless witness. The fact is that we have a kind of spontaneous inner dynamic of "non-acceptance" operative within each of us, to which we have even often been scrupulously trained. We either run away from our experience, or get afraid of it, or get guilty about it, or repress and suppress it—all various forms of "non-acceptance." How, I ask, do we *deal with* experience by first making a *tabula rasa* of it? Hence the absolutely indispensable need for first *consciously accepting* our very real experience; then we can effectively deal with this experience as genuine *Christians*.

If we have grasped what the New Testament so consistently and powerfully teaches on the distinctive note and character of being "Christian" or a "disciple of Christ" (we might call it the typically "Christian" criterion of discernment)—namely, to *give and surrender self* to the Lord,[17] that is, to become "free" for the Lord and, in him, for our brothers and sisters—we can now do precisely this in the very real experience which we have just consciously accepted. It would not be out of place to recall here that categorical Ignatian sentence in the book of the Exercises which we have quoted above, and which is, in fact, the entire dynamics of the Exercises in a nutshell: "Let everyone keep in mind that in all things that concern the spiritual life progress is in proportion to getting out of self-love, self-will, and self-interest" (*Spir. Exercises*, 189).

Having become existentially "free" in the here-and-now of our real experience, we are able to "find God" or be united with him in that very same real experience consciously accepted. We have, in effect, gone through the entire dynamics of the Exercises in concentrated form.

We believe, however, that there would be in all of this a highly significant "missing link" if we did not show how the concrete fruit of the actual personal experience of the Exercises in fact influences the regular daily practice of the "consciousness examen."

In my recently published work, *The Personal Vocation: Transformation in Depth Through the Spiritual Exercises*, to which I have already made reference earlier on, I have shown how every single one of us has in his or her "personal vocation," which is the deepest and most radical understanding of the "Election" of the Ignatian Exercises, his or her own unique way of giving and surrendering self in any human experience.[18] In other words, every single one of us has been gifted by the Lord with a *personal secret* of becoming and staying "free" in the midst of any and every human experience, gifted with a *unique secret and criterion of discernment* in the midst of all our human experience. In this way, the specific "Christian" step of the "Consciousness Examen" is for us, at the stage of having consciously accepted our real experience, to put on in depth the attitude of our "personal vocation," which will "free" us from ourselves to touch the Lord in and through that real concrete experience. Thus real everyday human experience, concrete everyday life, can in very truth become ceaseless prayer or union with God; the commonplace, run-of-the-mill, "ordinary" of everyday living can be the raw matter in and through which we discern the "extraordinary" because we are interiorly free or "docile to the Spirit."

Conclusion

We opened this chapter by remarking that the *living unity and integration* of contemplation and action, prayer and active apostolate, faith and life is the very heart of apostolic spirituality. We cannot help recalling in conclusion that powerful page of Paul the apostle—*the* apostle par excellence—in which he gives us one of the most profound insights into his spiritual life, his apostolic spirituality, and the way God formed him for the apostolate.

He tells us in 2 Cor 12 of his experience of "the thorn in the flesh" (v. 7) that was given him—most probably, as the majority of exegetes tell us today, a chronic sickness from the attacks of which Paul suffered periodically. Seeing in it an obstacle to his apostolic ministry—"a messenger of Satan to beat me" (v. 7)— Paul cries out three times to the Lord to be rid of it. How like his Master in the garden of Gethsemane! The answer Paul gets is that what he sees as an obstacle to his ministry is the precise, necessary, favorable and indispensable condition for the fruitfulness of his apostolic ministry; "for in weakness power reaches perfection" (v. 9)—a formulation in the most incisive terms of the fundamental law of all apostolate. What was a source of discouragement for Paul now becomes the precise motive of his confidence, so that he will burst out into a triumphant hymn boasting of his weaknesses, symbolized by his "thorn in the flesh." For in the apostle stripped of all reliance on human resources and emptied of all reliance on human supports, there incarnates itself the power of Christ—"when I am powerless, it is then that I am strong" (v. 10)—when he is empty of self and the more he is empty of self, that is interiorly free, the more he becomes the effective instrument of the power of God working in and through him.

What wonder that Paul can in and through the maelstrom of the chequered experiences of his apostolic life and ministry remain always "alive for God" (Rom 6:11)! No experience whatever becomes eventually an obstacle to "finding God." Who or what, then—if we might echo Paul's triumphant hymn to the all-conquering love of God which never ceases to come into our lives, that God who, Paul tells us a little earlier in the same passage: "...makes all things work out for the good"—"Who will separate us from the love of Christ? Trial, or distress, or persecution, or hunger, or nakedness, or danger, or the sword?...Yet in all this we are more than conquerors because of him who has loved us. For I am certain that neither death nor life, neither angels nor principalities, neither present nor the future, nor powers, neither height nor depth nor any other creature, will be able to separate us from the love of God that comes to us in Christ Jesus our Lord" (Rom 8:28, 35–39).

SUGGESTED READING

Alphonso, Herbert. *The Personal Vocation: Transformation in Depth Through the Spiritual Exercises*. Rome: Centrum Ignatianum Spiritualitatis, 1990; 6th ed. Anand: Gujarat Sahitya Prakash, 1993.

Aschenbrenner, George. "Consciousness Examen." *Review for Religious* 31(1972): 14–21.

———."A Check on Our Availability: The Examen." *Review for Religious* 39(1980): 321–24.

Bernard, Charles-André. *Teologia Spirituale*. 4th ed. Rome: Edizioni Paoline, 1993.

Courel, François, ed. *La vie et la doctrine spirituelle du Père Louis Lallemant*. Collection Christus no. 3. Paris: Desclée de Brouwer, 1959 (esp. IVème principe: "La docilité et la conduite du Saint Ésprit," 171–244).

Divarkar, Parmananda. *The Path of Interior Knowledge*. Rome/Anand: Centrum Ignatianum Spiritualitatis / Gujarat Sahitya Prakash, 1983.

English, John. *Spiritual Freedom: From an Experience of the Ignatian Exercises to the Art of Spiritual Direction*. Guelph: Loyola House, 1973.

Giuliani, Maurice. *Prière et Action*. Collection Christus no. 21. Paris: Desclée de Brouwer, 1966.

Green, Thomas H. *Weeds Among the Wheat: Where Prayer and Action Meet*. Notre Dame, Ind.: Ave Maria Press, 1984.

Lefrank, Alex. *Freedom for Service: Dynamics of the Ignatian Exercises as Currently Understood and Practised*. Anand: Gujarat Sahitya Prakash, 1989.

Chapter Eight

The Saint as Moral Paradigm

DONNA L. ORSUTO

The postmodern world presents particular challenges to authentic Christian discipleship. The apparent breakdown of a coherent moral or religious consensus which typifies postmodern culture necessitates a critical reflection on how Christians present and live the Gospel. In a time when abstract theories and ideas seem to have lost their compelling force,[1] it is not enough simply to explicate the demands of Christian discipleship. In and of themselves, they do not hold and attract followers to Christ. New modes of communication are necessary. The moral confusion and spiritual disorientation which characterize contemporary society cry out for the proclamation of the Good News. The problem is to find a mode of communication which is comprehensible to contemporary men and women; a language which responds to their often unarticulated religious yearning.

This chapter suggests that the most effective way to transmit the Good News is through the personal witness of disciples. Not only through their words, but most especially through their actions, they provoke a response in people. Mother Teresa of Calcutta, a woman whom many would consider a living "saint," exemplifies this point. Without a doubt, she has made and is making a powerful impact on contemporary society. What attracts people to her, though, is not so much what she says, but who she is and what she does. As an authentic disciple of Christ, she communicates the Good News with her life. She radiates

Christ's presence and draws people to God. In diverse situations over the centuries, people like Mother Teresa, including both the more restricted category of canonized saints and other exemplars, have embodied Christian values and ideals to such an extent that they have become moral paradigms. Their lives challenge others with the demands of Christian discipleship, but they do so in a pre-theoretical language that transcends mere theories and ideas.

Christian Discipleship in the World of Jurassic Park

This pre-theoretical communication is particularly important in postmodern society because of the pointed disillusionment with theories and ideas. In many ways, the epitome of the postmodern crisis is the story of "Jurassic Park." In the world of Jurassic Park, scientific experiments with DNA allow dinosaurs to come back to life in the rationally "controlled" environment of an island theme park. However, in a terrifying turn of events, the dinosaurs escape human mastery and wreak havoc. As in Jurassic Park, so in current society, theory no longer appears to have the capacity to bring order to the postmodern world.[2]

One does not have to embrace the current abandonment of theory that marks so much of contemporary philosophy to recognize that theory by itself does not bring about moral change in society. Past attempts to establish dialogue with secular culture on moral issues seem to have reached an impasse. The shift to postmodernity marks a recognition that the Church and the world no longer share a common set of moral values.[3] The Christian in postmodern society is similar to Kierkegaard's story of the clown in the burning village. As one author explains, when the clown tries in vain to convince the villagers of an impending fire, his words are not taken seriously because he is "ticketed and classified," so to speak, by his role:

> Whatever he does in his attempt to demonstrate the seriousness of the position, people always know in advance that he is in fact just—a clown. They are already familiar

with what he is talking about and know that he is just giving a performance which has little or nothing to do with reality.[4]

In this context, contemporary culture poses a serious challenge to Christians: how to present the Christian ideal of discipleship in a setting where moral theories seem to have lost their force.

One point is clear, theories in and of themselves rarely compel one to moral or religious conversion.[5] As John Paul II says, "people today put more trust in witnesses, than in teachers, in experience than in teaching, and in life and action than in theories."[6] Perhaps this is one of the reasons why he has beatified and canonized an unprecedented number of people during his pontificate.[7] In his most recent encyclical letter, *Veritatis splendor*, John Paul II specifically refers to the saints as moral paradigms: "By their eloquent and attractive example of a life completely transfigured by the splendor of moral truth, the martyrs and, in general, all the Church's Saints, light up every period of history by reawakening its moral sense."[8]

Who Are the Saints?

A. The Postmodern Philosophical Debate. Is the saint though an effective witness in postmodernity? In the field of moral philosophy, there are diverse opinions about who the saints are and their role as moral paradigms. This is exemplified in the exchange between Susan Wolf and Robert Adams. Wolf argues that saints, with their morally good actions, are unattractive as models because they seem bland and dull. Her three criteria for moral sainthood include the following: (1) every act of that person is "as morally good as possible"; (2) the person himself or herself is as "morally worthy as can be"; and (3) "one's life be dominated by a commitment to improving the welfare of others or of society as a whole."[9] Fulfilling these three criteria is such an all-consuming task that other "nonmoral virtues as well as many of the interests and personal characteristics" of a "healthy, well rounded richly developed character" would be excluded.

Consequently, the saint emerges as a "strangely barren" and boring person.[10] In critiquing Wolf's somewhat narrow perception of sainthood, Adams suggests that "actual saints" (and there actually *are* saints) are "immensely attractive" and "intensely interesting" to others. He insists that sainthood must ultimately be seen as a religious phenomenon; the central focus is the saint's relationship with God.[11] He stresses that "the substance of sainthood is not sheer willpower striving like Sisyphus (or like Wolf's Rational Saint) to accomplish a boundless task, but goodness overflowing from a boundless source."[12]

Another important contribution in the field of moral philosophy is Edith Wyschogrod's *Saints and Postmodernism*. She argues for a "hagiographical ethics" as a compelling alternative to reliance upon moral theory. Her ideas are quite complex and far beyond the scope of this study. Nevertheless, her definition of a saint, though much broader than the Christian understanding, does give some insight into the direction of her "hagiographical ethics." She defines

> the saint—the subject of hagiographic narrative—as one whose adult life in its entirety is devoted to the alleviating of sorrow (the psychological suffering) and pain (the physical suffering) that afflicts other persons without distinction of rank or group or, alternatively, that afflicts sentient beings, whatever the cost to the saint in pain or sorrow. On this view theistic belief may but need not be a component of the saint's belief system.[13]

Among her numerous contributions, she considers two major questions: how the saints exemplify "what moral lives are" and how they demonstrate concretely how "one might go about living a moral life."[14]

B. The Saints in the Christian Tradition. This chapter proposes to explore these two points specifically from a Christian perspective. In the Christian tradition, the saints are not the dull unfulfilled individuals described by Wolf; rather they are paradigms of human authenticity. The saints reflect human fulfillment par excellence. As Karl Rahner suggests, the saints are "initiators and the creative models of the holiness which happen to be right for, and is the task of, their particular age."[15] They also serve as teachers and models of Christian morality. Bernard Häring suggests that we should turn to the "magisterium of the saints" for guidance—they can teach us how to respond to the call of discipleship today.[16]

In the New Testament, the followers of Christ were called saints (Acts 9:13, 32, 41; Rom 1:7; 16:2; Phil 1:1).[17] They were set apart as a people or community for God alone. Over the centuries, the term gradually developed to refer specifically to certain deceased believers who were honored in a special way because of their faithful witness to Christ, even unto death (the martyrs) or because of their exceptional holiness.

In a broad sense, saints refer to those persons whose experience of intimate union with Christ so transforms them that they are conformed to his image and likeness. Their lives are transparent: in their being and acting, the divine love and presence shines through them to such an extent that others recognize this and look to them as paradigms of Christian discipleship. Because of their intimate communion with Christ and with all members of the Body, others are drawn to turn to them in intercession and veneration. Some, who through martyrdom or through the exercise of heroic virtue, whose writing has undergone careful scrutiny and who have been proven to be intercessors (through miracles), are officially recognized by the Roman Catholic Church as "blessed" or "saints."[18]

Since the martyr is the "highest mark of love,"[19] we shall use it as a specific example to show precisely how the saint is a moral paradigm. What does the martyr tell us about living a moral life? The word "martyr," which literally in Greek means "witness," represents the ideal of discipleship. From earliest times to today, the martyrs were honored as those who sacrificed their lives in an ultimate act of love and fidelity to Christ and his teaching:

Condemned, tortured, bloodied, and executed, martyrs were perceived by other Christians as entering in a graphic way into the dying of Jesus, and so into his rising. They were icons of Jesus Christ, awesome signs of the victory of his power in the face of the evil of this world.[20]

In the period from apostolic times to 312, an epoch interspersed with great persecution in the Church, the martyrs were perceived as authentic disciples. They were models for other Christians of how they should act when faced with hostility for their Christian faith. This is particularly evident in *The Acts of the Christian Martyrs*.[21] For example, in the moving account of "The Martyrdom of Saints Perpetua and Felicitas," Perpetua stands out as model of unwavering commitment to Christ. Despite pressure from her family and the pain of eventually being separated from her baby, she had only one reply to her pleading father:

"Father," said I, "do you see this vase here…"
"Yes, I do," said he.
And I told him: "Could it be called by any other name than what it is?"
And he said: "No."
"Well, so too I cannot be called anything other than what I am, a Christian."[22]

Sometimes in the romanticization of the early martyrs, the concrete reality of fear and isolation is overlooked. The readiness of Perpetua to sacrifice her life for her convictions in spite of the suffering that she endured surely poses a challenge to men and women of postmodern society. Though martyrdom is a gift to which few are called, part of the Christian vocation is to be ready to offer a "consistent witness" even in the midst of suffering and sacrifice.[23] As Lawrence Cunningham has noted:

The willingness to die for one's faith is the ultimate test of faith commitment. The threat of death is so powerful that it becomes the touchstone by which we measure what we hold as ultimate and nonnegotiable in life. What is it we would die for? Honor? Country? Family? Possessions? Love? When we read of the religious martyrs, they remind us—they test us—about the degree to which we have or have not accepted the discipleship of Jesus. They force us to ask: Would we go that far?[24]

The saint, and more specifically the martyr, exemplifies what the moral life is. The moral life is not simply following rules, it finds its meaning in a loving relationship with Christ, a relationship which shapes one's actions.

C. The Identification and Recognition of the Saints in Cult. The historical development of the cult of the saints is quite complex, and beyond the scope of this study. However, a brief review of salient points will demonstrate how the saints emerged as moral paradigms. Up until the beginning of the fourth century, the only persons who were venerated as saints were the martyrs.[25] Eventually, non-martyrs or "confessors" were recognized for their heroic witness to Christ in the midst of persecution. With the cessation of persecution, other outstanding holy persons, especially monks and virgins, were venerated.

Peter Brown has shown that in Late Antiquity the saints were seen as exemplars who re-presented Christ. In that period, the aim and effect of the *imitatio Christi* was to make "Christ present by one's own life in one's own age and region."[26] As John S. Hawley so succinctly suggests when introducing Brown's essay:

> Their personhood was the crux of the morality they taught—often implicitly rather than discursively—and what they sought to imitate and perfect was no specific aspect of the life of Jesus…but the unfallen Adam that waits to be rediscovered within us all. They were not examples typifying aspects of the whole, they were convincingly the whole; as exemplars they contrasted markedly to a world of shards and fallen fragments by which they were surrounded. They showed the way through to a level of being so coherent that in contrast to the dimness or at best reflected glory of ordinary existence it seemed able to generate its own light. Hence the language of luminosity pervades descriptions of them. Their impact was registered in "flashes of signal light" and "shining visions," not in what is usually meant by moral instruction.[27]

During this period, the cult of the saints was very much a grass-roots movement under the authority of the local bishops, and it was only in the tenth century that the Pope became more officially involved.[28] Eventually, it became more centralized and the process of recognition of saints developed into a formal and somewhat complex ecclesiastical exercise.

The formal process leading to canonization has been developing since the Middle Ages. Key moments in the development include the formation in 1588 by Sixtus V (1585–90) of the Congregation of Rites which took responsibility for the identification of saints, the complex procedure developed by Urban VIII (1623–44), Prospero Lambertini's (Benedict XIV, 1740–58) study of beatification and canonization, the critical study of the saints by the Jesuit Bollandists which was started in the seventeenth century by Jean Bolland (and particularly inspired by Leribert Rosweyde, 1569–1629), the 1917 Code of Canon Law, and the formation of the Congregation for Causes of the Saints in 1969, which was formerly a part of the Congregation of Rites.[29] The most recent reform, which simplified the process, took place in 1983 with John Paul II's Apostolic Constitution, *Divinus perfectionis magister.*[30]

Throughout the development of the canonization process, the main purpose was and is to provide models of holiness. Holiness, which is nothing other than union with Christ in love, necessarily has an effect on one's moral actions. This is evident when considering the two traditional categories of saintliness: namely, martyrdom and heroic virtue. Martyrdom, considered "the highest gift and supreme test of love," is of course the apex of Christian heroism.[31] Other candidates for beatification or canonization, though not gifted with martyrdom, must exercise heroicity of virtue.[32] Heroic or exceptional virtue implies that one is so radically transformed by God's own love as to live profoundly and in an exemplary way the theological virtues of faith, hope, and charity and the four cardinal moral virtues of prudence, justice, fortitude, and temperance. Whether for the martyr or others who have exemplified heroic virtue, the operative word is love: the key is to live a life of exceptional love toward God and neighbor.

D. Lex Orandi, Lex Credendi, Lex Vivendi. The liturgical prayer of the Church regularly presents us with the challenge of the saints as models for Christian living. For example, Vatican II's "Constitution on the Sacred Liturgy" says that the Church proposes the martyrs and other saints to the faithful "as examples" who draw all to God.[33] Further, in the first Eucharistic preface for Holy Men and Holy Women I (The Glory of the Saints), the Church prays:

> Father, all powerful and ever living God…you are glorified in your saints, for their glory is the crowning of your gifts. *In their lives on earth, you give us an example.* In our communion with them, you give us their friendship. In their prayer for the Church you give us strength and protection. *This great company of witnesses spurs us on to victory* to share their prize of everlasting glory, through Jesus Christ our Lord…[34]

Likewise, the second Eucharistic preface, Holy Men and Holy Women II (On the Activity of the Saints), the faithful are encouraged to look to the saints as models:

> You (Father) renew the Church *in every age by raising up men and women outstanding in holiness, living witnesses of your unchanging love. They inspire us by their heroic lives, and help us by their constant prayers to be the living sign of your saving power.*[35]

The proper of saints in the *Roman Sacramentary* emphasizes the particular ways that each martyr or other saint acts as an exemplar. This specific focus is accompanied by a prayer that the faithful would be inspired to act in the same way. For example, on January 28, when the Roman Catholic Church celebrates the memorial of St. Thomas Aquinas, the opening prayer is as follows: "God our Father, you *made Thomas Aquinas known for his holiness and learning. Help us to grow in wisdom by his teaching, and in holiness by imitating his faith….*" Again on June 3, the feast of Charles Lwanga and Companions, we pray, "Father, you have made the blood of the martyrs the seed of Christians. *May the witness of St. Charles and his companions and their loyalty to Christ in the face of torture inspire countless men and women to live the Christian faith."* Both of these, and other similar opening prayers for saints, begin by recognizing the source of the exemplary life, namely God. Then a particular characteristic of the saint's witness is emphasized (for St. Thomas Aquinas, his holiness and learning; for St. Charles and his companions, their loyalty to Christ in the face of persecution and death). Finally, it is accompanied by the petition that the faithful might be inspired by the example of the saint. There is a movement from *lex orandi* to *lex credendi* to *lex vivendi*: prayerful contact with the saint's witness which is proclaimed in the liturgy is meant to transform one's life.

What the Moral Life Is: Discipleship

So far we have determined who the saints are and that they are presented as models both in the historical development of cult and in liturgy. In light of this, the obvious question is: precisely how do the saints show us what the moral life is? The answer is simple, yet profound: *they do so by manifesting to us what it means to be a disciple of Christ.*

In recent years, the theme of discipleship has been proposed as a "powerful paradigm for Christian living."[36] In his book, *A Church to Believe In: Discipleship and the Dynamics of Freedom*, Avery Dulles, S.J. argues persuasively that an appropriate model of the Church for this age is that of the "Church as a Community of Discipleship." He introduces this proposal by quoting from John Paul II's first encyclical *Redemptor hominis*:

> Therefore, if we wish to keep in mind this community of the people of God, which is so vast and so extremely differentiated, we must see first and foremost Christ saying in a way to each member of the community: "Follow me." It is *the community of the disciples*, each of whom in a different way—at times very consciously and consistently, at other times not very consciously and very consistently—is

following Christ. This shows also the deeply "personal" aspect and dimension of this society.[37]

In light of this focus on the Church as a community of disciples, two particular questions arise: what do we mean by discipleship and how is it a manifestation of the moral life? How can those who have "very consciously and consistently" followed Christ serve as models for the rest of us?

Of the 90 times that the word "disciple" occurs in the New Testament, seventy-nine are in the gospels.[38] Though each of the four gospels has its own particular point of view,[39] they converge on the description of discipleship as a personal and intimate relationship with and total adherence to Jesus Christ (Mk 8:34–38; Mt 16:24–26; Lk 9:23–26; Jn 15:1–12). The moral life is best characterized by discipleship which has the following three characteristics. Firstly, this relationship begins with *a divine initiative*: Jesus calls individuals to a personal and intimate relationship with him (Mk 3:14 "as his companions"), an invitation that is often heard in the midst of ordinary activities. Secondly, discipleship implies *a radical break with the past and a new commitment to Jesus' way of being and acting*. Thirdly, *the experience of discipleship empowers one to carry on Jesus' mission*, even in the midst of persecution.

After the death, resurrection, and ascension of Jesus, the notion of discipleship changed dramatically. As Dulles notes:

For the first time a community of disciples existed without the visible presence of the Master. One might imagine that in that case the apostles would replace their absent Lord, and would themselves become Christ to their followers. To some extent this did occur. They spoke in his name, so that Jesus could say of them, "Whoever hears you hears me" (Lk 10:16). "As the Father has sent me, I send you" (Jn 20:21). Paul could write to his Corinthian converts: "Be imitators of me as I am of Christ" (1 Cor 11:1). But the disciples never really took the place of Jesus, who alone remained, in the full sense, Master and Lord.[40]

Paul's attitude is fundamental for understanding the challenge of discipleship in the early Church. While each follower was called into an intimate and personal relationship with the Risen Lord, certain members of the community, like Paul himself, were exemplars of how concretely this could be done in diverse circumstances. It is for this reason Paul could say, "Imitate me as I imitate Christ" (1 Cor 11:1).

Learning To Live the Moral Life: Saints as Paradigms

This scripturally-rooted focus on discipleship is particularly relevant while facing the challenge to be a Christian in a post-Christian and postmodern society. The call to discipleship is just as definite today as it was when Jesus was walking along the Sea of Galilee. Today as in the past, discipleship implies that there is no cheap grace.[41] Total adherence to Jesus means following him and incarnating his way of being and acting in one's own life. The challenge is to respond to this call in diverse historical and cultural situations. The saints stand out as exemplars of Christian discipleship by incarnating gospel values existentially in time and space.[42]

In considering the saints as paradigms of discipleship, it is important to understand in what sense they are an example. As John S. Hawley notes:

> The key term is *example*, a word whose meanings diverge in two directions that are only distantly related. In one sense an example is an instance, an illustration, a case in point. In the other, an example is not a subset of something larger but a paradigm that sets the shape for a series of imitative phenomena that follow in its wake. It is a model, a proto-type, not merely an example but an exemplar. Both these usages help us to state the moral impetus so often present in hagiographical traditions. On the one hand, saints can be examples *of* something, or even of someone; on the other, they can be examples *to* someone.[43]

Indeed, as Lawrence Cunningham notes, "the life of the saint should act as a parable. It should shock us into a heightened and new sense of God's presence (and judgment) in our own lives."[44] We might add, the lives of the saints should shock us into embracing the demands of Christian discipleship.

If not only individuals, but the Church as a whole is a community of disciples, it must be stressed that this community includes also Mary, the "perfect disciple,"[45] and the communion of saints, those who have constantly and consistently responded to the call of discipleship. As noted above, discipleship is intimately intertwined with one's personal relationship with and adherence to Jesus Christ. More than anyone else, Mary and the saints have responded to this challenge. They are icons of Christ. They mirror Christ by taking on his way of being and acting in diverse historical and cultural situations.[46]

Conclusion

The saints have not only gone before us as models to be imitated, they are also our companions on the journey. This is a profound truth: as part of the body of Christ, we do not have to go on the journey alone. There are a host of companions, living and dead, who share with us, who celebrate with us, who help us on our way. Indeed, we invoke the saints in liturgy as companions of prayer. "It is for that reason we pray at the liturgy to have 'some share in the fellowship of your apostles and martyrs'; that we beg to praise God 'in union with them,' and why, finally, we are bold to ask 'to share in the inheritance of all your saints.' "[47]

SUGGESTED READING

Brown, Peter. *The Cult of the Saints: Its Rise and Function in Latin Christianity*. Chicago: The University of Chicago Press, 1981.

Conn, Walter. *Christian Conversion: A Developmental Interpretation of Autonomy and Surrender*. New York: Paulist Press, 1986.

Cunningham, Lawrence. *The Meaning of Saints*. San Francisco: Harper and Row, 1980.

DeLooz, Pierre. "Towards a Sociological Study of Canonized Sainthood in the Catholic Church." Translated by Jane Hodgkin. In *Saints and Their Cults: Studies in Religious Sociology, Folklore and History*. Edited by Stephen Wilson. Cambridge: Cambridge University Press, 1983, 189–216.

Dulles, Avery. *A Church to Believe In: Discipleship and the Dynamics of Freedom*. New York: Crossroad, 1982.

Hawley, John S., ed. *Saints and Virtues*. Berkeley: University of California Press, 1987.

Molinari, Paul. "Martyrdom: Love's Highest Mark and Perfect Conformity to Christ." *The Way Supplement* 39(1980): 14–24.

Molinari, Paul and Peter Gumpel. "Heroic Virtue: The Splendour of Holiness." *The Way Supplement* 39(1980): 25–34.

Segovia, Fernando F., ed. *Discipleship in the New Testament*. Philadelphia: Fortress Press, 1985.

Tavard, George. "The Veneration of Saints as an Ecumenical Question." *One in Christ* 26(1990): 40–50.

Thompson, William. *Fire and Light: The Saints and Theology*. New York/Mahwah: Paulist Press, 1987.

Whalen, Michael. "The Saints and Their Feasts: An Ecumenical Exploration." *Worship* 63(1989): 194–209.

Notes

CHAPTER ONE

1. Van A. Harvey uses the phrase "field-encompassing" to describe the interdisciplinary character of historical study. See *The Historian and the Believer: The Morality of Historical Knowledge and Christian Belief* (Philadelphia: The Westminster Press, 1966), 54–59.

2. Fyodor Dostoyevsky, *The Brothers Karamazov*, trans. David Magarshack (London: Penguin Books, 1958; reprint, 1982), 14 (page references are to reprint edition).

3. Ibid., 77.

4. James M. Gustafson, "Spiritual Life and Moral Life," *Theology Digest* 19(no. 4, 1971): 298.

5. Although treated in a different order, the full definitions are found in Servais (Th.) Pinckaers, *Les sources de la morale chrétienne: sa méthode, son contenu, son histoire*, Études d'éthique chrétienne, no. 14 (Fribourg, Suisse: Éditions Universitaires, 1985), 15–18.

6. For the emergence of these disciplines, see A. Vacant, E. Mangenot, and É. Amann, eds. *Dictionnaire de théologie catholique* (Paris: Librairie Letouzey et Ané, 1923–), s.v. "Théologie," by M.-J. Congar.

7. Dostoyevsky, *The Brothers Karamazov*,199.

8. For a summary of this process, see Andrew Louth, *Discerning the Mystery: An Essay on the Nature of Theology* (Oxford: Clarendon Press, 1983), 1–16. See also Hans Urs von Balthasar, "Theologie und Heiligkeit," chap. in *Verbum Caro: Skizzen zur Theologie I* (Einsiedeln: Johannes Verlag, 1960), 195–201.

9. For a definition of spiritual theology, see Jordan Aumann,

Spiritual Theology (London: Sheed and Ward, 1980), 22. The specific description of spirituality as a field-encompassing discipline comes from Sandra M. Schneiders, "Spirituality in the Academy," *Theological Studies* 50(1989): 692.

10. Walter H. Principe, "Toward Defining Spirituality," *Studies in Religion/Sciences religieuses* 12(1983): 136. For the influence of spirituality on the study and practice of religion, see Patrick Sherry, *Spirit, Saints and Immortality* (Albany: State University of New York Press, 1984), 3–4; Cheslyn Jones, "Note on 'Spirituality'" in *The Study of Spirituality*, eds. Cheslyn Jones, Geoffrey Wainwright, and Edward Yarnold (Cambridge: University Press, 1986; second impression, 1992), xxiv–xxvi (page references are to second impression); Hans Urs von Balthasar, "Spiritualität," chap. in *Verbum Caro: Skizzen zur Theologie I* (Einsiedeln: Johannes Verlag, 1960), 226–44.

11. Principe, "Toward Defining Spirituality," 135–36. See also Michael Downey, ed., *The New Dictionary of Spirituality* (Collegeville, Minn.: The Liturgical Press, 1993), s.v. "Spirituality, Christian," by Walter H. Principe.

12. Francis Schüssler Fiorenza, "Theology in the University," *The Council of Societies for the Study of Religion Bulletin* 22(no. 2, 1993): 37.

13. See Acts 15:1–35.

14. For the difficulty of pinpointing Gnostic origins, see Helmut Koester, *Introduction to the New Testament*, vol. 1, *History, Culture, and Religion of the Hellenistic Age* (Philadelphia: Fortress Press, 1982), 382–88.

15. See, for example, the description of Gnostic morality in Hans Jonas, *The Gnostic Religion*, 2d ed. (Boston: Beacon Press, 1963), 270–77.

16. William Tabbernee, "Dissenting Spiritualities in History," *The Way* 28(1988): 138.

17. For the rationalistic character of Arianism, see Johannes Quasten, *Patrology*, vol. 3, *The Golden Age of Patristic Literature* (Westminster, Md.: Christian Classics, Inc., 1960; reprint, 1983), 8 (page references are to reprint edition).

18. Hubert Jedin, ed., *History of the Church* (New York: The Seabury Press, 1980), vol. 2, *The Imperial Church from Constantine*

to the Early Middle Ages, by Karl Baus, Hans-Georg Beck, Eugen Ewig, and Hermann Josef Vogt, trans. Anselm Biggs, 3–16.

19. When dealing with Neoplatonic thought both authors adopt what is consistent with Christianity and seek to amend what is not. For a brief summary of their Christian adaptations of Neoplatonic thought, see Étienne Gilson, *History of Christian Philosophy in the Middle Ages* (London: Sheed and Ward, 1955; reprint, 1985), 70–85 (page references are to reprint edition).

20. David Knowles, *Christian Monasticism* (New York/Toronto: McGraw-Hill, 1969; reprinted, 1972, 1979), 37 (page references are to the 1979 reprint edition). See also G. Jacquemet, ed., *Catholicisme: hier, aujourd'hui, demain* (Paris: Letouzey et Ané, 1948–), s.v. "Bénédictins," by Dom G. Marié.

21. David Knowles, *The Evolution of Medieval Thought* (New York: Random House, 1962), 32. See also G. Bonafede, "L'influsso del pensiero di Sant'Agostino nel medioevo," *Italia francescana* 30(1955): 10–18, 65–72.

22. Katherine Fischer Drew, "Introduction," in *The Lombard Laws,* trans. idem, with a Foreword by Edward Peters (Philadelphia: University of Pennsylvania Press, 1973; reprint, 1981), 1 (page references are to reprint edition).

23. A good description of this expansion is provided by Lester K. Little, *Religious Poverty and the Profit Economy in Medieval Europe* (Ithaca, N.Y.: Cornell University Press, 1978), 218–19.

24. For Latin Christianity's recovery of Aristotle during the twelfth and thirteenth centuries, see Brian Tierney and Sidney Painter, *Western Europe in the Middle Ages, 300–1475,* 3d ed. (New York: Alfred A. Knopf, 1978), 386–88. See also Wilhelm Totok, *Handbuch der Geschichte der Philosophie,* vol. 2, *Mittelalter* (Frankfurt am Main: Vittorio Klostermann, 1973), s.v. "Die Hochscholastik: 'Aristotelismus'; 'Erste Verwertung des Aristoteles.'"

25. For a comparison of monastic and scholastic theologies, see B.P. Gaybba, *Aspects of the Medieval History of Theology* (Pretoria: University of South Africa, 1988), 52–57. See also Jean Leclercq, *The Love of Learning and the Desire for God,* 3d ed., trans. Catharine Misrahi (New York: Fordham University Press, 1982), 193–202.

26. "Neque enim quaero intelligere ut credam, sed credo ut

intelligam." Anselm of Canterbury, *Proslogion*, chap. 1 in *Anselmi opera omnia* (Stuttgart-Bad Cannstatt: Friedrich Frommann Verlag, 1984) 2:100.

27. For a summary of Ockham's metaphysics, see P. Boehmer, "The Metaphysics of William Ockham," *Review of Metaphysics* 1(1948): 59–86; for his ethics, see Lucan Freppert, *The Basis of Morality according to William Ockham* (Chicago: Franciscan Herald Press, 1988), 141–70.

28. "Plurality is never to be posited without necessity." William of Ockham, *In I Sent.*, d. 27, q. 2 resp. in *Opera philosophica et theologica* (St. Bonaventure, N.Y.: St. Bonaventure University, 1979), 2:205.

29. For the influence of nominalism on Counter Reformation moral theology, see J.-M. Aubert, "Morale et casuistique," *Recherches de science religieuse* 68(1980): 171–73.

30. For the basic tenets of Deism, see Philip P. Wiener, ed., *Dictionary of the History of Ideas* (New York: Charles Scribner's Sons, 1973), s.v. "Deism," by Roger L. Emerson.

31. For a short summary of Kant's turn toward the subjective, see Benedict M. Ashley, *Theologies of the Body: Humanist and Christian* (Braintree, Mass.: The Pope John Center, 1985), 215–16. See also J. Manzano, "El problema de la objectividad en el conocimento sensitivo, según Kant," *Antonianum* 48(1973): 248–67.

32. For a helpful description of "postmodernism," see Agnes Cunningham, "Modernity/Postmodernity: The State of the Question for Contemporary Catholic Theology," in *The Catholic Theological Society of America: Proceedings of the Forty-Sixth Annual Convention (Atlanta, June 12–15, 1991)*, ed. Paul Crowley (Santa Clara, Calif.: The Catholic Universty of America, 1991), 156. See also Downey, ed. *The New Dictionary of Spirituality*, s.v. "Postmodernity," by Michael Downey.

33. The notion of theological reflection as a threefold interplay of the concepts of God, the human person, and the world is taken from N. Max Wildiers, *The Theologian and His Universe: Theology and Cosmology from the Middle Ages to the Present* (New York: The Seabury Press, 1982), 1.

34. The claim that rationality is a concept with a history comes

from Alasdair MacIntyre, *Whose Justice? Whose Rationality?* (Notre Dame, Ind.: University of Notre Dame Press, 1988), 9.

35. Dostoyevsky, *The Brothers Karamazov*, 296.

CHAPTER TWO

1. See above Dennis J. Billy, "The Unfolding of a Tradition," 11–15.

2. Augustine, *The Confessions*, bk. 8, chap.12.

3. Hilda Graef, *Edith Stein: Zeugnis des Vernichteten Lebens*, 5th ed. (Frankfurt am Main: Josef Knecht, 1979), 44–45.

4. Graef, *Edith Stein*, 47; cf. Edith Stein, *Life in a Jewish Family 1891–1916*, trans. Josephine Koeppel (Washington, D.C.: ICS Publications, 1986), 420.

5. Michael J. Buckley, "The Rise of Modern Atheism and the Religious *Epoché*," in *The Catholic Theological Society of America: Proceedings of the Forty-Seventh Annual Convention (Pittsburgh, June 11–14, 1992)*, ed. Paul Crowley (Santa Clara, Calif.: The Catholic University of America, 1992), 76.

6. For more on Las Casas, see Ph. André-Vincent, *Bartolomé de Las Casas, prophète du Nouveau Monde* (Paris: Tallendier, 1980); Marrianne Mahn-Lot, *Bartolomeo de las Casas e i diritti degli indiani* (Milano: Jaca Book, 1985); Gustavo Gutiérrez, *Las Casas: In Search of the Poor of Jesus Christ* (Maryknoll, N.Y.: Orbis, 1993).

7. He was, at this time, probably in minor orders. He was ordained a priest some years later. Mahn-Lot, *Bartolomeo*, 23.

8. Gutiérrez, *Las Casas*, 46.

9. Mahn-Lot, *Bartolomeo*, 29; Gutiérrez, *Las Casas*, 46.

10. André-Vincent, *Bartolomé*, 26; Gutiérrez, *Las Casas*, 46.

11. Mahn-Lot, *Bartolomeo*, 33; Gutiérrez, *Las Casas*, 47.

12. Gutiérrez, *Las Casas*, 61–64; André-Vincent, *Bartolomé*, 26.

13. Gutiérrez, *Las Casas*, provides an extended account. Cf. Ronald G.Musto, *The Catholic Peace Tradition* (Maryknoll, N.Y.: Orbis, 1986), 140.

14. Brian Tierney, "Aristotle and the American Indians— Again," *Cristianesimo nella storia* 12(191): 302, 316–17.

15. Michael Sievernich, "Social Sin and Its Acknowledgment," *Concilium* 190(April, 1987): 52.

16. Buckley, "The Rise," 77.

17. "Secretum meum mihi." Graef, *Edith Stein*, 44.

18. For example, see the suggested readings on pp. 47-48.

19. Bernard Lonergan, "Theology in Its New Context," in *A Second Collection*, eds. William F.J. Ryan and Bernard J. Tyrell (Philadelphia: The Westminster Press, 1974), 67. Cited in Michael L. Rende, *Lonergan on Conversion: The Development of a Notion* (Lanham, Md.: University Press of America, 1991), ix.

20. Bernard Lonergan, *Method in Theology* (New York: The Seabury Press, 1972), 129.

21. Ibid., 338.

22. "Logic makes but a sorry rhetoric with the multitude; first shoot round corners and you may not despair of converting by a syllogism." John Henry Newman, *An Essay in Aid of a Grammar of Assent* (New York: Doubleday, 1955), 90; quoted in Lonergan, *Method*, 338.

23. Lonergan, *Method*, 105.

24. Ibid., 107.

25. Graef, *Edith Stein*, 45.

26. Lonergan, *Method*, 240.

27. Ibid., 242.

28. See Charles E. Curran and Richard A. McCormick, *Readings in Moral Theology*, no. 2, *The Distinctiveness of Christian Ethics* (New York: Paulist Press, 1980).

29. Charles Taylor, *Sources of the Self: The Making of Modern Identity* (Cambridge, Mass.: Harvard University Press, 1989), 138.

30. Augustine, *Confessions*, bk. 8, chap. 9; English translation from F.J. Sheed, *The Confessions of St. Augustine* (London: Sheed and Ward, 1944), 141.

31. Augustine, *Confessions*, bk. 7, chap. 21.

32. Thomas Aquinas, *S.th.*, I–II, q. 109, a. 8; Alasdair MacIntyre, *Whose Justice? Which Rationality?* (Notre Dame, Ind.: University of Notre Dame Press, 1988), 181.

33. Aquinas, *S.th.*, I–II, q. 113, a. 3; Jean Claude Dhôtel, *La conversion à l'évangile* (Paris: Centurion, 1975), 63.

34. Aquinas, *S.th*, III, q. 85, a. 5, resp.

35. See Charles Davis, "Lonergan's Appropriation of the Concept of Praxis," *New Blackfriars* 62(1981): 114–26.

36. Gustavo Gutiérrez, *A Theology of Liberation*, revised ed. (London: SCM Press, 1988), 118.

37. Ibid., 118.

38. Sievernich, "Social Sin," 52–63.

39. John Paul II, *Centesimus annus* (Vatican City: Libreria Editrice Vaticana, 1991), no.38.

40. Ibid.

41. Taylor, *Sources*, 91.

42. MacIntyre, *Whose Justice?*, 361.

43. Josef Pieper, *Überlieferung: Begriff und Anspruch* (Munich: Kösel Verlag, 1970), 90. Pieper refers to the ideas of Jung.

44. William James, *The Varieties of Religious Experience* (New York: Macmillan, 1967), 175–76.

45. Buckley, "The Rise," 78.

46. On the link between conversion and fundamental option, see Karl Rahner, ed., *Encyclopedia Teologica: Sacramentum Mundi* (Brescia: Morcelliana, 1974), s. v. "Conversione," by Karl Rahner.

47. Newman, *Grammar*, 92.

48. Graef, *Edith Stein*, 45.

49. Bernard Häring, *Free and Faithful in Christ*, vol. 1, *General Moral Theology* (New York: Seabury, 1978), 216.

50. Gutiérrez, *Las Casas*, 6. This work is a thorough and insightful study of Las Casas' theological contribution.

51. She wrote a work on the State, *Eine Untersuchung über den Staat*, 1925.

52. Graef, *Edith Stein*, 66.

53. Ibid., 65.

54. Karl Rahner, ed., *Encyclopedia Teologica, Sacramentum Mundi* (Brescia: Morcelliana, 1974), s.v. "Conversione," by Karl Rahner.

55. B.C. Butler, "Bernard Lonergan and Conversion," *Worship* 49(1975): 333.

56. Ibid., 332.

57. Lonergan, *Method*, 338.

58. Ibid.

59. In stressing the place of narrative and tradition, I have

developed an aspect which is not so evident in Lonergan's writing on conversion.

60. This does not mean "canonized" saints only. Edith Stein was declared blessed in 1987.

61. See George P. Schner, "The Appeal to Experience," *Theological Studies* 53(1992): 40–59.

62. See David Tracy, *The Analogical Imagination* (New York: Crossroad, 1981), 167.

63. Gustavo Gutiérrez, *Las Casas: In Search of Jesus Christ*, trans. Robert R. Barr (Maryknoll, N.Y.: Orbis, 1993).

64. Ibid., 45.

65. Billy, "The Unfolding," 15–24.

66. Ibid., 13–14.

67. Graef, *Edith Stein*, 127.

68. Ibid., 304.

69. Edith Stein, *Life*, 435.

70. Graef, *Edith Stein*, 301.

71. Ibid.

72. Ibid., 302.

73. Gutiérrez, *Las Casas*, 326.

CHAPTER THREE

1. A. Caron, "Canon Law and Moral Theology," *The Jurist* 22(1962): 319, where he cites Thomas Aquinas, *S.th.*, I, q. 1, a. 3.

2. For a good example of the separation of the different theological disciplines and the subsequent loss of a coherence among them, see E. Farley, *Theologia: The Fragmentation and Unity of Theological Education* (Philadelphia: Fortress Press, 1983). Much has been written, especially among educators, as a commentary on this work and its implications.

3. G. Lindbeck, "Spiritual Formation and Theological Formation," *Theological Education, Supplement* 1(1988): 22–23.

4. E. McDonagh, *The Making of Disciples. Tasks of Moral Theology* (Wilmington, Del.: Michael Glazier, 1982), 22.

5. J.C. Hough, Jr. and J.B. Cobb, Jr., *Christian Identity and Theological Education* (Chico, Calif.: Scholars Press, 1985), 116.

6. See Congregation for Catholic Education, "Norms Implementing the Apostolic Constitution *Sapientia cristiana*, 29 April 1979," no. 51, Appendix II, nos. 15 and 26 in *Acta Apostolicae Sedis* 71(1979): 513, 520–21.

7. B.J. Fleischer, "The Ignatian Vision for Higher Education: Practical Theology," *Religious Education* 88(1993): 259. This idea of practical theology has been widely discussed among educators. As examples of writings in this area, see Hough and Cobb, *Christian Identity*; L.S. Mudge and J.N. Poling, eds., *Formation and Reflection. The Promise of Practical Theology* (Philadelphia: Fortress Press, 1987). In the latter book, the editors explain the direction that practical theology should take: "What is the relation between 'theology' as an academic discipline and living, worshiping, serving communities of faith. Despite good intentions that it should be otherwise, many today would say that little relationship exists" (p. xiii). Practical theology should bridge the gap between academic knowledge and a lived vibrant faith.

8. H.R. Niebuhr, D.D. Williams, and J.M. Gustafson, *The Advancement of Theological Education* (New York: Harper,1957), 133.

9. D.J. Hall, "Theological Educational Character Formation," *Theological Education, Supplement* 1(1988): 67–88.

10. C.M. Wood, "'Spiritual Formation' and 'Theological Education,'" *Religious Education* 86(191): 556–57.

11. J.M. Gustafson, "The Vocation of the Theological Educator," *Theological Education, Supplement* (1987): 64–65.

12. See Vatican II, *Lumen gentium*, no. 40 in Austin Flannery, ed., *Vatican II*, 397.

13. Ibid., no. 41, p. 398.

14. John Paul II, *Sapientia christiana*, no. 4 in *Origins* 9(1979): 36.

15. Ibid., no. 25, p. 39.

16. John Paul II, *Ex corde Ecclesiae*, no. 22 in *Origins* 20(1990): 270.

17. Congregation for the Doctrine for the Faith, *Donum veritatis*, no. 7 (Vatican City: Libreria Editrice Vaticana, 1990), 7.

18. Ibid., no. 9, p. 8.

19. T.P. Walters, "Instructional Objectives, Catechesis and the Future," *Religious Education* 85(1990): 85.

20. Wood, "'Spiritual Formation,'" 556.

21. J. A. Coriden, "The Canonist's Vocation and a New Church Order," *The Jurist* 51(1991): 67–68.

22. Gustafson, "The Vocation," 65–66.

23. Niebuhr, Williams, and Gustafson, *The Advancement*, 57.

24. Ibid., 141.

25. This is not to say that teachers who do not begin with a sense of vocation and who do not bring an active faith to their teaching are necessarily poor teachers. In fact, they might be good teachers, but something will be lacking in what the students learn. As G. Lindbeck notes: "Although good theology is possible without spiritual maturity (or even belief), it is generally better…when it is done by the spiritually mature, by those who are skilled in the practice of the faith." See "Spiritual Formation," 19.

26. T.H. Groome, "The Spirituality of the Religious Educator," *Religious Education* 83(1988): 14.

27. Ibid., 14–18.

28. Ibid., 19.

29. Ibid., 20.

30. Ibid., 9.

31. M. Trainor, "Images of the Faith Educator," *Religious Education* 86(1991): 285–86.

32. Niebuhr, Williams, and Gustafson, *The Advancement*, 142.

33. Gustafson, "The Vocation," 60. While this may sound good, to put it into practice is extremely difficult. As the same author notes (p. 61): "How does one affirm the reality of God and how are we to live in relation to God in the light of interpretations of the world and life in the world that pervade our culture? On what foundations do we ground moral values and principles and how do we defend them in a morally relativistic culture? How do we establish the grounds for human freedom and accountability in the light of more deterministic explanations of behavior?" To answer these questions is beyond the scope of this article, but they will need to be considered by the teacher who wishes to teach a theology that courageously embraces the world.

34. Dom Sighard Kleiner, *Serving God First. Insights on the Rule*

of St. Benedict, Cistercian Series, no. 83, trans. James Scharinger (Kalamazoo, Mich.: Cistercian Publications, 1985): 167.

35. There are many editions of the Benedictine Rule as well as commentaries on the Rule. One recent one is: A. de Vögué, *Ce que dit saint Benoît: une lecture de la Règle* (Abbaye de Bellefontaine, 1991).

36. Ibid., 169–70.

37. Esther de Waal, *Seeking God. The Way of St. Benedict* (Collegeville, Minn.: The Liturgical Press, 1984), 108.

38. J. Louis Martyn, "Focus: Theological Education or Theological Vocation?" in J.Y. Holloway and W.D. Campbell, eds. *Callings!* (New York: Paulist Press, 1974), 252.

CHAPTER FOUR

1. Karl Rahner, "Christian Living Formerly and Today," chap. in *Theological Investigations*, vol. 17 (London/New York: Darton, Longman and Todd/Herder and Herder, 1971), 15.

2. See, for example, F. Roberti and P. Palazzini, eds. *Dizionario di teologia morale*, 3rd ed. (Rome: Studium, 1961), s.v. "Preghiera," by L. Bender; F.J. Connell, *Outlines of Moral Theology* (Milwaukee: Bruce, 1953), 142–43; M. Zalba, *Theologiae moralis compendium*, vol. 1 (Madrid: La Editorial Católica, 1958), 536–38.

3. See, for example, F. Compagnoni, G. Piana, and S. Printero, eds., *Nuovo dizionario di teologia morale* (Milan: San Paolo, 1990), s.v. "Preghiera," by G. Piana.

4. H. Boelaars, "La preghiera nell'opera della salvezza," *Studia moralia* 9(1971): 233–36.

5. S. Bastianel, *Prayer in Christian Moral Life* (Slough: St. Paul, 1988). See also B. Häring, *Road to Relevance* (Staten Island, N.Y.: Alba House, 1970), 113–15.

6. See, for example, AA.VV. *Ascesi della preghiera*. Fiamma viva, no. 2 (Rome: Teresianum Institute of Spirituality, 1961); E. Ancilli, ed. *La preghiera. Bibbia, teologia, esperienze storiche*, 2d ed., 2 vols. (Rome: Città Nuova, 1990).

7. See, for example, D. Dorr, *Spirituality and Justice* (Dublin/Maryknoll, N.Y.: Gill and Macmillan/Orbis, 1984), 217–55.

8. John Damascene, *De fide orthodoxa*, 3:24 in *Fathers of the Church*, 37:378 (*PG* 94:1089).

9. Gregory of Sinai, *Chapters*, 113 (*PG* 150:1280); see K.Ware, *The Power of the Name. The Jesus Prayer in Orthodox Spirituality* (London: Marshall Pickering, 1989).

10. Augustine, *Enarr. in Ps. 37:14* (PL 36:404); see idem, *Serm.* 152:1 (*PL* 38:820); G. Corcoran, *Prayer and St. Augustine*, Living Flame, no. 25 (Dublin: Carmelite Centre of Spirituality, 1986), 18–20.

11. See J. Meyendorff, "Theosis in the Eastern Christian Tradition," in L. Dupré and D.E. Saliers, eds., *Christian Spirituality*, vol. 3, *Post Reformation and Modern World Spirituality* (New York: Crossroad, 1989; London: SCM, 1990), 470–76; Marcel Viller, Charles Baumgartner, André Rayez, eds., *Dictionnaire de spiritualité ascétique et mystique, doctrine et histoire* (Paris: Beauchesne, 1937–94), s.v. "Divinization," by E. de Places et al. (esp. I.-H. Dalmais on the Greek Fathers).

12. Athanasius, *De incarnatione*, 54 (*PG* 25:192).

13. See, for example, F. Giardini, "The Growth Process of Christian Prayer Life," *Angelicum* 69(1992): 389–421.

14. R. Studzinski, "Prayer and Life," *Chicago Studies* 31(1992): 26.

15. Bernard Lonergan, *Method in Theology* (London: Darton, Longman and Todd, 1972), 104–07.

16. John of the Cross, *Ascent of Mount Carmel*, 2:5,5 in K. Kavanaugh and O. Rodriguez, trans. *The Collected Works of St. John of the Cross* (Washington, D.C.: ICS Publications, 1973), 117. See also J.V. Rodríguez, "Trinidad y vida mística en San Juan de la Cruz," *Estudios Trinitarios* 16(1982): 226–30.

17. T. Spidlík, *The Spirituality of the Christian East. A Systematic Handbook*, Cistercian Studies 79 (Kalamazoo, Mich.: Cistercian Publications, 1986), 103–07.

18. Ibid., 183–85.

19. S. Noffke, ed., *The Prayers of Catherine of Siena* (New York/Ramsey, N.J.: Paulist Press, 1983), passim.

20. X. Pikaza, "La preghiera, esperienza trinitaria," in *La preghiera cristiana. Sintesi* (Rome: Borla, 1991), 182–91.

21. Vatican II, *Ad gentes divinitus*, no. 2 in Flannery, ed., *Vatican Council II*, 814.

22. Epiclesis of confirmation rite.

23. Thomas Aquinas, *Summa c. gent.*, bk. 4, chaps. 21–22.

24. See Vatican II, *Lumen gentium*, nos. 39–42 in Flannery, ed., *Vatican Council II*, 396–402.

25. Marcel Viller, Charles Baumgartner, André Rayez, eds., *Dictionnaire de spiritualité ascétique et mystique, doctrine et histoire* (Paris: Beauchesne, 1937–94), s.v. "Contemplation," by J. Lebreton et al.

26. Thomas Aquinas, *S. th*, II–II, q. 180, aa.3–4.

27. A. Cunningham, "Forms of Prayer in Christian Spirituality," *Chicago Studies* 15(1976): 99.

28. *Das betrachtende Gebet*, 4th ed. (Einsiedeln: Johannes, 1977); English trans. *Prayer* (San Francisco: Ignatius Press, 1986).

29. Quoted in Igumen Chariton of Valmo, *The Art of Prayer. An Orthodox Anthology* (London/ Boston: Faber and Faber, 1966), 51.

30. Teresa of Avila, *The Way of Perfection*, 21:6 in K. Kavanaugh and O. Rodriguez, trans., *The Collected Works of St. Teresa of Avila*, vol. 2 (Washington, D.C.: ICS Publications, 1980), 119.

31. H. Blommestijn, "Discovering the Self and the World through the Eyes of God. A Selective Reading of 'The Spiritual Canticle,' " *Studies in Spirituality* 3(1993): 173–99.

32. D. Mongillo, "Vita morale e vita mistica," *Rivista di teologia morale* 97(1993): 117–23; see also A. de Marino, "Vita morale e spirituale," *Rivista di teologia morale* 24(1992): 231–37.

33. See, for example, S.P. Morgan, "Prayerfulness in America," *Chicago Studies* 20(1981): 237–52.

34. R. Chandler, *Understanding the New Age* (Dallas/Milton Keynes, UK: Word Publishing, 1988); R. Berzosa Martínez, "'New Age' un nuevo reto a la teología," *Lumen* 41(1992): 266–80; A. Cavadi, "La dimensione mistica fra 'New Age' e nichilismo," *Sapienza* 45(1992): 391–407.

35. J. Drane, *What Is the New Age Saying to the Church?* (London: Marshall Pickering, 1991), 38.

36. See J. A. Wiseman, "From Sunday to Weekday: On Praying at All Times," *Chicago Studies* 31(1992): 13–22; L.J. Cameli,

"Preaching and the Teaching of Prayer in Parishes,"*Chicago Studies* 31(1992): 3–12.

CHAPTER FIVE

1. See Vatican II, *Lumen gentium*, no. 40 in Flannery, ed., *Vatican Council II*, 397.

2. Peter E. Fink, ed. *The New Dictionary of Sacramental Worship* (Collegeville, Minn.: The Liturgical Press, 1990), s.v. "Liturgy and Christian Life," by Enda McDonagh.

3. *Enchiridion documentorum instaurationis liturgicae I* (1963–1973) [hereafter *EDIL*], ed. Reiner Kaczynski (Torino: Marietti, 1976), 4 [my translation].

4. This understanding of the liturgy is perhaps best expressed in the definition given by Cyprian Vagaggini: "The liturgy is the complexus of the sensible signs of things sacred, spiritual, invisible, instituted by Christ or by the Church; signs which are efficacious, each in its own way, of that which they signify; by which signs God (the Father by appropriation), through Christ the Head and Priest, and in the presence of the Holy Spirit, sanctifies the Church, and the Church as a body, in the presence of the Holy Spirit, uniting herself to Christ her Head and Priest, through Him renders her worship to God (the Father by appropriation)." Cyprian Vagaggini, *Theological Dimensions of the Liturgy: A General Treatise on the Theology of the Liturgy*, 4th ed., trans. Leonard J. Doyle and W.A. Jurgens (Collegeville, Minn.: The Liturgical Press, 1976), 25.

5. *EDIL*, 5 [my translation].

6. *EDIL*, 4 [my translation].

7. *EDIL*, 471 [my translation].

8. *EDIL*, 486 [my translation].

9. *EDIL*, 740–41 [my translation].

10. *EDIL*, 742–43 [my translation].

11. See Peter L. Berger and Thomas Luckmann, *The Social Construction of Reality: A Treatise in the Sociology of Knowledge* (New York: Doubleday, 1966); Peter L. Berger, *The Sacred Canopy: Elements of a Sociological Theory of Religion* (New York: Doubleday,

1967); idem, *A Rumor of Angels: Modern Society and the Rediscovery of the Supernatural* (New York: Doubleday, 1969).

12. See Stephen Crites, "The Narrative Quality of Experience," *Journal of the American Academy of Religion* 39(1971): 295–311; John Shea, *Stories of God* (Chicago: Thomas More, 1978); idem, *Stories of Faith* (Chicago: Thomas More, 1980); *Why Narrative? Readings in Narrative Theology*, ed. Stanley Hauerwas and L. Gregory Jones (Grand Rapids: Eerdmans, 1989).

13. Paul J. Wadell, "What Do All Those Masses Do for US? Reflections on the Christian Moral Life and the Eucharist," in *Living No Longer for Ourselves: Liturgy and Justice in the Nineties*, eds. Kathleen Hughes and Mark R. Francis (Collegeville, Minn: The Liturgical Press, 1991), 154.

14. *Missale Romanum ex decreto Sacrosancti Oecumenici Concilii Vaticani II instauratum auctoritate Pauli Pp. VI promulgatum. Editio Typica Altera* [hereafter *MR* 1975] (Città del Vaticano: Libreria Editrice Vaticana, 1975), 820 [my translation].

15. *MR* 1975:823 [my translation].

16. *MR* 1975: 837 [my translation].

17. *The Roman Missal: The Sacramentary* (New York: Catholic Book Publishing Co., 1985), 1128.

18. Ibid., 555.

CHAPTER SIX

1. Jordan of Saxony, Letter 25 in *To Heaven with Diana*, trans. Gerald Vann (New York: Pantheon Books, 1960), 104.

2. Mary Gordon, *The Company of Women* (New York: Ballantine Books, 1980), 275; quoted in Paul Wadell, *Friendship and the Moral Life* (Notre Dame, Ind.: University of Notre Dame Press, 1989), 160.

3. See Daniel A. Helminiak, *Spiritual Development: An Interdisciplinary Study* (Chicago: Loyola University Press, 1987), esp. chap. 3. In this chapter, Helminiak examines "maturational" and "psychological" approaches to human development; he also presents (pp. 72–73) a well-ordered table/comparison of eight prominent thinkers.

4. See Erik H. Erikson, *Childhood and Society*, 2d ed. (New York: W. W. Norton, 1963), esp. 247–74.

5. Donald Evans, *Spirituality and Human Nature* (Albany: State University of New York Press, 1993).

6. The story of Narcissus and Echo is recounted in Ovid, *Metamorphoses*, trans. Mary M. Innes (New York: Penguin Books, 1955), 83–87.

7. Evans, *Spirituality and Human Nature*, 52.

8. For a more recent summary and expansion of the discussion about theories of moral development, see Charles M. Shelton, *Morality of the Heart: A Psychology for the Christian Moral Life* (New York: Crossroad, 1990). Shelton himself proposes "empathy" as the critical virtue/skill for the moral life.

9. See especially, Lawrence Kohlberg, *The Philosophy of Moral Development*, vol. 1, Essays on Moral Development (San Francisco: Harper and Row, 1981), esp. 6–28.

10. See Carol Gilligan, *In a Different Voice: Psychological Theory and Women's Development* (Cambridge, Mass.: Harvard University Press, 1982); Cynthia Crysdale, "Gilligan and the Ethics of Care: An Update," *Religious Education* 20(1994): 21–29.

11. Joseph A. Komonchak, Mary Collins, and Dermot Lane, eds., *The New Dictionary of Theology* (Wilmington, Del.: Michael Glazier, 1987), s.v. "Trinity," by Edmund Dobbin.

12. See Richard of St. Victor, "Book Three of the Trinity," in *Richard of St. Victor*, The Classics of Western Spirituality Series, trans. Grover A. Zinn (New York: Paulist Press, 1979), 371–97.

13. Michael J. Himes and Kenneth R. Himes, *Fullness of Faith: The Public Significance of Theology* (New York/Mahwah, N.J.: Paulist Press, 1993), 56.

14. John Paul II, *Dominicum et vivificantem*, no. 10 (Rome: Vatican Polyglot Press, 1986), 18.

15. This is an adaptation of one of Edward Schillebeeckx's "constant" qualities of the human person in his work *Christ: The Experience of Jesus as Lord* (New York: Crossroad, 1981), 736–37.

16. Stefano de Fiores and Tullo Goffi, eds. *Nuevo Diccionario de Espiritualidad*, trans. Augusto Guerra (Madrid: Ediciones Paulinas, 1983), s.v. "Horizontalismo/verticalismo," by Gian Carlo Vendrame [the English translation is my own].

17. Ibid.

18. Early patristic authors like Irenaeus treated "image" and "likeness" distinctively. He identified the former with the human person as a rational and free being and the latter with the right relationship which humanity possessed with God and all creation before the Fall. See Michael Downey, ed., *The New Dictionary of Spirituality* (Collegeville, Minn.: The Liturgical Press, 1993), s.v. "Imago Dei," by Mary Catherine Hilkert. Although that distinction may be helpful in other discussions, I am not following it here.

19. Joseph A. Komonchak, Mary Collins, and Dermot Lane, eds., *The New Dictionary of Theology* (Wilmington, Del.: Michael Glazier, 1987), s.v. "Anthropology, Christian," by Michael Scanlon.

20. Gilbert Meilaender, *Friendship: A Study in Theological Ethics* (Notre Dame, Ind.: University of Notre Dame Press, 1981), 8.

21. Ibid., 11.

22. Aristotle, *Nichomachean Ethics*, bk. 8, chap. 3; English translation from J.A.K. Thomson, *The Ethics of Aristotle: Nichomachean Ethics*, revised by Hugh Tredennick with an Introduction and Bibliography by Jonathan Barnes (New York: Penguin Books, 1976), 263. St. Thomas Aquinas concurs with Aristotle in this assessment when he writes: "...not all love has the character of friendship, but that only which goes with well wishing, namely when we so love another as to will what is good for him. For if what we will is our own good, as when we love wine or a horse or the like, it is a love not of friendship but of desire" (*S.th.*, II–II, q. 23, a. 1, resp.).

23. Wadell, *Friendship*, 152.

24. Augustine, *The Confessions*, bk. 4, chap. 6; English translation from John K. Ryan, *The Confessions of St. Augustine* (Garden City, N.Y.: Image Books, 1960), 100.

25. Ibid., bk. 4, chap. 8, p. 101.

26. Ibid., bk. 4, chap. 12, p. 104.

27. Meilaender, *Friendship*, 16.

28. Augustine, *Confessions*, bk. 4, chap. 10; English translation from Ryan, *The Confessions of St. Augustine*, 102.

29. Ibid.

30. Adele M. Fiske, *Friends and Friendship in the Monastic Tradition* (Cuernavaca, Mexico: Centro Intercultural de Documentación, 1970), 2–3; quoted in Meilaender, *Friendship*, 20.

31. See Aquinas, *S.th.*, II–II, q. 24, a. 9, resp.

32. Ibid.

33. Ibid., I–II, q. 22, a. 2, ad 1m.

CHAPTER SEVEN

1. See Vatican II, *Gaudium et spes*, esp. nos. 36–39 in Flannery, ed., *Vatican Council II*, 935–38.

2. Pierre Teilhard de Chardin, *Le milieu divin: essai de vie intérieure* (Paris: Éditions du Seuil, 1957).

3. This phrase "contemplation in action" has become well-known because of a celebrated passage in which Father Jerome Nadal, close associate and companion of St. Ignatius Loyola, comments on the graces of prayer granted to "Father Ignatius": "This manner of praying was granted to Father Ignatius by a great and very special privilege; and also this further grace, that in all things and actions and conversations he experienced and contemplated the presence of God and had a lively feeling for spiritual reality—*being contemplative in his very action* ('*simul in actione contemplativus*'). His own favorite way of putting it was: *God must be found in all things*" (*Annotationes in Examen*, c. 4: *Monumenta Nadal*, 5:162–63).

4. This was St. Ignatius' "own favorite" phrase, as the previous note makes clear. He has enshrined it in the Jesuit Constitutions as his most perfect formulation of the true ideal of apostolic prayer: "All should make diligent efforts to keep their intention right, not only in regard to their state of life but also in all particular details…Further, they should often be exhorted *to seek God Our Lord in all things*, stripping off from themselves the love of creatures to the extent that this is possible, in order to turn their love upon the Creator of them, *by loving Him in all creatures and all of them in Him….*" (*Constitutions*, 288). For Ignatius' recurrent use of this his favorite phrase, see *Autobiography*, 99; *Monumenta Ignatiana, Epistolae*, 3:502, 510.

5. We may take as examples: for *priests*: Pope John Paul II, *Pastores dabo vobis* of March 25, 1992, nos. 24–26; for *religious*: Sacred Congregation for Religious and Secular Institutes, *The Contemplative Dimension of Religious Life* of May 1980, nos. 4–7; for the *laity*: Pope John Paul II, *Christifideles Laici* of December 30, 1988, no. 17.

6. This is the refrain of one of the songs in the Indian poet-laureate Rabindranath Tagore's charming collection of poems, "Gitanjali" (= song offerings), which in 1930 won him the Nobel Prize for Literature. The opening verses of this song read: "Have you not heard his silent steps? / He comes, comes, ever comes. / Every moment and every age, every day and every night / He comes, comes, ever comes." See *Gitanjali* (London: Macmillan, 1967), 36–37.

7. Not without profound reason does Vatican II, in chapter 8 of *Lumen gentium* on the mystery of Mary (nos. 52–69), present our Lady as the type and figure not only of the Church, but of the Christian spiritual life in its growth towards perfection: at the Annunciation, which is the concentrated summing-up of the whole mystery of Mary which only unfolds itself progressively thereafter, God takes the initiative of breaking into Mary's life; and Mary's response is, with all the power and energy of her freedom, to *actively allow* God to do in her as he wished: "Be it done to me according to your word." See Flannery, ed., *Vatican Council II*, 413–23.

8. Ignatius openly acknowledges that God led him through his experience, "treating him…just as a schoolmaster treats a child whom he is teaching" (*Autobiography*, 27).

9. When asked by Luis Gonçalves da Câmara about how he had composed the Exercises (da Câmara, to whom Ignatius recounted his life-story, that is, how "God had led him"), Ignatius replied "that he had not composed the Exercises all at once, but that when he noticed some things in his soul and found them useful, he thought they might be useful to others, and so he put them in writing…" (*Autobiography*, 99).

10. Elsewhere, in my recently published book [*The Personal Vocation: Transformation in Depth Through the Spiritual Exercises* (Rome: Centrum Ignatianum Spiritualitatis, 1990), 15–36], I have

shown that the "Election" of the Ignatian Exercises is, in its most profound and radical sense, a person's unrepeatable *uniqueness*, the "name" by which God calls that person—that is, his or her truest and deepest "self"—the secret of unity and integration at the heart of that person's life, his or her unique God-given meaning in life, centered in Christ Jesus. This is what I call the "personal vocation."

11. As is well known, this is John of the Cross' expression for the summit of, or total, detachment. See, for example, his *Ascent of Mount Carmel*, bk. I, chap. 3, nos. 1–2; chap. 4, nos. 3–4; chap. 6, no. 4; chap. 13, no. 6; bk. II, chap. 4, no. 5.

12. The companions of Ignatius who lived and worked with him in Rome have many such anecdotes to recount. Among them was Luis Gonçalves da Câmara, the Minister of the Professed House in Rome. See his *Mémorial*, nos. 214–15 in Collection Christus, no. 20 (Paris: Desclée de Brouwer, 1966).

13. See Alphonso, *The Personal Vocation*, 53–54, 63–65.

14. Lk 4:1–2 is here very revealing and instructive: "Jesus, *full of the Holy Spirit*, returned from the Jordan, and was *conducted by the Spirit* into the desert for forty days, where he was tempted by the devil." When Jesus is "full of the Spirit" and "conducted by the Spirit," then precisely is he most open and vulnerable to the attacks of the counter-spirit, who seeks to vitiate and falsify his whole messianic mission, which he has just received in his baptism (Lk 3:21–22).

15. For a more detailed explanation and understanding of the "Consciousness Examen," see Alphonso, *The Personal Vocation*, 63–73.

16. See Thomas Green, *Weeds Among the Wheat* (Notre Dame, Ind.: Ave Maria Press, 1984), 98ff.

17. Mt 16:24 ("If a man wishes to come after me, he must deny his very self, take up his cross, and begin to follow in my footsteps") is only one statement among many others—but this in lapidary fashion—of what it means to be authentically a "disciple of Christ."

18. See n. 10 above (esp. 36–37, 52–54, 70–71).

CHAPTER EIGHT

1. See *Anti-Theory in Ethics and Moral Conservatism*, eds. Stanley G. Clark and Evan Simpson (Albany: State University of New York Press, 1989).

2. I got this image of "Jurassic Park" from Timothy Radcliff, "Challenges to Our Mission in the First World," *Sedos Bulletin* 26(1994): 148–50. He uses it to contrast the world of Jurassic Park, a world of violence, competitive consumerism, isolation, and fatalism with the way of Christ. As he notes (p. 148) and as I agree, there are also positive elements of contemporary society which should be taken into account including "a cherishing of the individual, human rights, a tolerance of those who are different, etc."

3. On this theme, see Walter Kasper, *The God of Jesus Christ* (New York: Crossroad, 1987), 3–75.

4. Joseph Ratzinger, *Introduction to Christianity*, trans. J.R. Foster (San Francisco: Ignatius Press, 1990), 15–16. As Ratzinger notes, the story was popularized by Harvey Cox's book, *The Secular City* (New York: Macmillan, 1966).

5. Walter Conn, *Christian Conversion: A Developmental Interpretation of Autonomy and Surrender* (New York: Paulist Press, 1986), esp. 158–268. In speaking of Thomas Merton's conversion experience, he comments (p. 179): "A life of self-transcendence does not grow and flourish into conversion without the nourishment of a strong model." He is speaking of Merton's personal friends, but it seems that the idea can be broadened to consider saints as exemplars.

6. John Paul II, *Redemptoris missio. Encyclical Letter on the Permanent Value of the Church's Missionary Mandate* (Vatican City: Libreria Editrice Vaticana, 1991), 42.

7. See Patrick de Laubier, "Sociologie des saints," *Revue thomiste* 91(1991): 34–67; Jean Evanou, "Les saints et bienheureux proclamés par Jean Paul II (1978–1988)," *Esprit et vie* 99(1989): 200–07; Kenneth Woodward, *Making Saints* (New York: Simon and Schuster, 1990): 120–22.

8. John Paul II, *Veritatis splendor. Encyclical Letter The Splendor of Truth Shines* (Vatican City: Libreria Editrice Vaticana, 1993), 93.

9. Susan Wolf, "Moral Saints," *Journal of Philosophy* (1982): 419–39, esp. 420.

10. Ibid., 421.

11. Robert Adams, "Saints," *Journal of Philosophy* 81(1984): 392–401.

12. Ibid., 398. See also Owen Flanagan, *Varieties of Moral Personality* (Cambridge, Mass.: Harvard University Press, 1991).

13. Edith Wyschogrod, *Saints and Postmodernism* (Chicago/London: The University of Chicago Press, 1990), 34.

14. Ibid., 4. For a description of postmodernism and a summary and critique of Wyschogrod's position, see David Matthew Matzko, "Postmodernism, Saints and Scoundrels," *Modern Theology* 9(1993): 19–36.

15. Karl Rahner, "The Church of the Saints," chap. in *Theological Investigations*, vol. 3, *The Theology of the Spiritual Life* (New York: The Seabury Press, 1974), 100.

16. Bernard Häring, *Free and Faithful in Christ*, vol. 2, *The Truth Will Set You Free* (Middlegreen Slough: Saint Paul's Publications, 1979), 218. For introducing me to this theme in Häring's writings, I am grateful to William Thompson, *Fire and Light: The Saints and Theology* (New York: Paulist Press, 1987), 28n. 4. From a Methodist tradition, Stanley Hauerwas also recognizes the importance of saints. In "Ethics and Ascetical Theology," *Anglican Theological Review* 61(1979), 98, he says: "Attending to the lives of the saints is for Christians the means of moral growth on which all other aspects of moral life depend." For this and further references to Hauerwas' position that the saints are models of the Christian life who represent "what we are about," see Kevin O'Neil, *What Should We Be? A Study of Stanley Hauerwas's Christian Tradition-Dependent Character Ethics* (S.T.D. diss., Accademia Alfonsiana, 1989), 256–58. For a survey of recent research on saints, see Lawrence Cunningham, "A Decade of Research on the Saints: 1980–1990," *Theological Studies* 53(1992): 517–33.

17. G. Kittle and G. Friedrich, eds., *Theological Dictionary of the New Testament* (Grand Rapids: Eerdmans, 1964–76), s.v. "Hagios," by Otto Procksch and Karl G. Kuhn.

18. For a history of the process of canonization, see William J. McDonald, gen. ed., *New Catholic Encyclopedia* (New York:

McGraw-Hill, 1967), s.v. "Canonization of Saints, History and Procedure," by Paul Molinari. The process was simplified in 1983 as we shall indicate further in the text.

19. See Vatican II, *Lumen gentium*, no. 42 in Flannery, ed.,*Vatican Council II*, 401; Paul Molinari, "Martyrdom: Love's Highest Mark and Perfect Conformity to Christ," *The Way Supplement* 39(1980): 14–24; *Nuovo Dizionario di Spiritualità*, 1978 ed., s.v. "Martire."

20. Elizabeth A. Johnson, "Saints and Mary," in *Systematic Theology, Roman Catholic Perspective*, ed. Francis Schüssler Fiorenza and John P. Galvin (Minneapolis: Fortress, 1991), 2:149.

21. *The Acts of the Christian Martyrs*. Introduction, texts, and translations by Herbert Musurillo (Oxford: Clarendon Press, 1972). See also W.H.C. Frend, *Martyrdom and Persecution in the Early Church: A Study from the Maccabees to Donatus* (Garden City, N.Y.: Doubleday, 1967).

22. *The Acts of Christian Martyrs*, 109.

23. John Paul II, *Veritatis splendor*, 93.

24. Lawrence S. Cunningham, *The Catholic Heritage* (New York: Crossroad, 1983), 23.

25. Agostino Amato, "Culto e canonizzazione dei santi nell'antichità cristiana," *Antonianum* 52(1977): 38–80, esp. 38–43. Also important for the early period is the excellent study by Peter Brown, *The Cult of the Saints: Its Rise in Latin Antiquity* (Chicago: University of Chicago Press, 1981).

26. Peter Brown, "The Saints as Exemplar in Late Antiquity," in *Saints and Virtues*, ed. John S. Hawley (Berkeley: University of California Press, 1987), 7.

27. Hawley, ed., *Saints and Virtues*, xv.

28. Johnson, "Saints and Mary," 2:147. In 993, Pope John XV was the first pope to canonize a saint. See also Michael Downey, ed., *The New Dictionary of Catholic Spirituality* (Collegeville, Minn.: The Liturgical Press, 1993), s.v. "Saints, Communion of," by Shawn Madigan.

29. See Christopher O'Donnell, ed., *Encyclopedia of the Church* (Collegeville, Minn.: The Liturgical Press, 1995), s.v. "Saints" by Christopher O'Donnell; William J. McDonald, gen. ed., *New Catholic Encyclopedia* (New York: McGraw-Hill, 1967), s.v.

"Bollandist," by P. Roche; Pierre DeLooz, "Towards a Sociological Study of Canonized Sainthood in the Catholic Church," trans. Jane Hodgkin in *Saints and Their Cults: Studies in Religious Sociology, Folklore and History*, ed. Stephen Wilson (New York: Cambridge University Press, 1983), 186–216.

30. John Paul II, *Divinus perfectionis magister, Acta Apostolicae Sedis* 75(1983); 349–55. The English translation of this document by Robert J. Sarno as well as "Norms to Be Observed by Bishops in the Causes of Saints" and the "General Decree," both documents of the Congregation for the Causes of the Saints, is published in *New Laws for the Causes of the Saints* (Rome, 1983). For a commentary and guide to the new legislation, see Fabijan Veraja, *Le cause di canonizzazione dei santi* (Vatican: Libreria Editrice Vaticana, 1992). On how the new legislation affects diocesan inquiries, see Robert J. Sarno, "Diocesan Inquiries Required by the Legislator in the New Legislation for the Causes of Saints," (J.C.D. diss., Gregorian University, 1988).

31. See Vatican II, *Lumen gentium*, no. 42 in Flannery, ed. *Vatican Council II*, 401; Molinari, "Martyrdom," 14–24.

32. Paul Molinari and Peter Gumpel, "Heroic Virtue: The Splendour of Holiness," *The Way Supplement* 39(1980): 25–34.

33. See Vatican II, *Sacrosanctum concilium*, no. 104 in Flannery, ed., *Vatican Council II*, 29.

34. *The Roman Missal: The Sacramentary* (New York: Catholic Book Publishing Co., 1985), 511. In this and subsequent quotations, the emphasis is mine. The focus on saints as models is also a helpful approach in ecumenical dialogue; see Michael Whalen, "The Saints and Their Feasts: An Ecumenical Exploration," *Worship* 63(1989): 194–209; George Tavard, "The Veneration of Saints as an Ecumenical Question," *One in Christ* 26(1990): 40–50.

35. *The Roman Missal: The Sacramentary*, 513.

36. See Keith J. Egan, "The Call of the Laity to a Spirituality of Discipleship," *The Jurist* 47(1987): 71–85. In light of the post-Vatican II era and the new Code of Canon Law, Egan suggests that the most appropriate spirituality of the laity is precisely a spirituality of discipleship.

37. John Paul II, *Redemptor hominis*, March 4, 1991, no. 21 as

quoted in Avery Dulles, *A Church to Believe In: Discipleship and the Dynamics of Freedom* (New York: Crossroad, 1992), 7 [emphasis mine].

38. David Noel Freedman, ed. in chief, *The Anchor Bible Dictionary*, 1st ed. (New York: Doubleday, 1992), s.v. "Disciple, Discipleship," Hans Weder.

39. See Fernando F. Segovia, ed., *Discipleship in the New Testament* (Philadelphia: Fortress Press, 1985).

40. Dulles, *A Church to Believe In*, 9.

41. Ibid., 10.

42. Lawrence Cunningham, *The Meaning of Saints* (San Francisco: Harper and Row, 1980), 2.

43. Hawley, "Introduction" in *Saints and Virtues*, xiii.

44. Cunningham, *Saints*, 79.

45. Mary is also referred to as the prototype of the "believer-disciple." See Dulles, *A Church to Believe In*, 9. For a further development of Mary's discipleship, especially as developed in Luke's Gospel, see Raymond E. Brown et al., *Mary in the New Testament* (New York/Mahwah, N.J.: Paulist Press, 1978), 105–77.

46. Cunningham, *Saints*, 75.

47. Lawrence Cunningham, *Catholic Prayer* (New York: Crossroad, 1989), 141.

Index of Names[1]

Abraham 85
Adam 133
Adams, Robert 129
Alphonso, Herbert v, 4, 6, 112
Alphonsus Liguori 68
Aristotle 12, 20, 103, 104, 105, 106,
Athanasius of Alexandria 70
Augustine of Hippo 19, 20, 32, 36, 38, 42, 70, 107, 108

Balthasar, Hans Urs von 75
Benedict of Nursia 62, 63
Benedict XIV 134
Berger, Peter 90
Billy, Dennis J. iii, 2, 5, 6, 9
Bolland, Jean 134
Bonaventure of Bagnoregio 21
Brown, Peter 133
Buckley, Michael 34

Catherine of Siena 73
Cunningham, Lawrence 132, 139

d'Andolo Diana 97
Donne, John viii
Dostoyevsky, Fyodor 2, 9, 12, 29
Drane, John 78
Dulles, Avery 136, 137

Erikson, Erik 99
Evans, Donald 99

Felicitas 132
Fiske, Adele 108
Freud, Sigmund 23

Gilligan, Carol 100
Gordon, Mary 98
Gregory of Sinai 69
Gregory the Great 19
Groome, T. H. 59, 60
Gutiérrez, Gustavo 37, 44

Häring, Bernard 68
Hawley, John H. 133, 138
Hervas, Juan, Bishop 77
Husserl, Edmund 32

---

[1] Excludes Notes and Suggested Readings.